D1236681

# THRIVING LATINA
# ENTREPRENEURS
# IN AMERICA

# THRIVING LATINA ENTREPRENEURS IN AMERICA

Written by
## Maria de Lourdes Sobrino

With
Mirna Medina

an imprint of New Win Publishing
a division of Academic Learning Company, LLC

Published by WBusiness Books,
an imprint of New Win Publishing,
a division of Academic Learning Company, LLC
9682 Telstar Ave. Suite 110, El Monte, CA 91731
www.WBusinessBooks.com

Cover Design by Gary Baltazar, Jr.

ISBN 10: 0-8329-5007-6
ISBN 13: 978-0-8329-5007-0

Manufactured in the United States of America
11  10  09  08  07        1  2  3  4  5

**Library of Congress Cataloging-in-Publication Data**

Sobrino, Maria de Lourdes, date,
  Thriving Latina entrepreneurs in America/Maria de Lourdes Sobrino.
  p. cm.
  Includes bibliographical references and index.
  ISBN 978-0-8329-5007-0 (alk. paper)
  1. Hispanic American businesswomen. I. Title.

HD6054.4.U6S66 2007
338'.040820973—dc22
                    2007029262

# Dedication

To the most important women in my life,
my mother Alicia and my daughter Monica.

# Contents

# Foreword

I have known and admired Maria de Lourdes Sobrino for many years. I had the honor of recognizing her as the "Woman of the Year" when I was the Chairman of the Latin Business Association (LBA) in 1998. In 2002, while I was the Administrator of the U. S. Small Business Administration, I had the privilege of introducing her to my boss, President George W. Bush, at the Economic Forum in Waco, Texas, where she was a representative of America's small business.

Lulu established Lulu's Dessert in 1982. It has consistently been ranked among the largest and fastest-growing Hispanic businesses in the United States, and Lulu has been called "the queen of ready-to-eat gelatin and a force in the surging number of Hispanic entre-preneurs," in *USA Today.* But there is more to Lulu's story, and to the success of Lulu's Dessert, than has been previously revealed: It is a story of success that is part of a larger story—the story of how Latina Entrepreneurs are transforming themselves, their industries, and the American business landscape.

Today, nearly 10.4 million firms are owned by women, employing more than 12.8 million people and generating $1.9 trillion in sales. For the past two decades, women-owned firms have continued to grow at around two times the rate of all firms. As with small business overall, the fastest growing segment of women-owned small business is Latina. These businesses are becoming a force in the marketplace.

By any measure, Maria de Lourdes Sobrino has been a trendsetter and certainly ahead of her time. She arrived into the U.S. market from Mexico in the 1980s with her Groups and Conventions Company and then, due to economic changes in Mexico, had to find a new niche. Her response was to create a new category of food product using her mother's recipe: ready-to-eat gelatin desserts. Lulu succeeded in capturing a significant share of the growing Hispanic market before the long-established and better-financed companies that followed her.

Lulu's success is not only remarkable because of her vision; it is remarkable because she acted upon her vision, against all odds. As a newly arrived immigrant she embarked upon a manufacturing endeavor in the food industry, which is arguably not only one of the most regulation-intensive industries, it is also one of the most competitive industries.

Her vision and her insights were the reason she was one of the first of many successful entrepreneurs I interviewed for a book I have written—*The Engine of America: The Keys to Small Business Success From Entrepreneurs Who Have Made It!*—and she certainly has made it.

Lulu has a special passion as an entrepreneur. She has decided to write her first book not only to inspire others through her story, knowledge, and experience, but also to share the inspiring stories of seven other remarkable Latina Entrepreneurs. They each have magnificently inspirational stories of turning great ideas into booming businesses. These Latinas would like to make a difference by opening the doors to the next generation of entrepreneurs. They have succeeded by overcoming all of the obstacles they have faced as female entrepreneurs, and thus have made a tremendous difference in their communities.

The main purpose of this book is to empower others to showcase their entrepreneurial talents by seeing these examples of successful Latinas.

It is a goal I share and applaud.

Hector Barreto
Chairman, The Latino Coalition
http://www.thelatinocoalition.com/
Former Administrator, U.S. Small Business Administration
Washington, D.C.
May 2007

# Acknowledgements

I am grateful to my parents Arturo and Alicia for being the greatest mentors in my life, and for setting such an incredible example. After all, my mother provided me with the foundation for my business, for it was her recipe of gelatin dessert that gave birth to Lulu's Dessert. Thank you to my brother Arturo and my sisters Cristina, Yolanda, and Alicia who have always been an important part of my life. My brother-in-law Luciano and my sister-in-law Elsa—I thank them for being part of such a close-knit family. To my nephews and nieces, Carlos, Francisco, Arturo, Fabian, Abraham, Luciano, Arturo Jr., Rodrigo, Patricio, Ana Alicia, Mariana, and Perla—I am very proud of the next generation of entrepreneurs in my family, I am glad they have followed in my footsteps.

To my amazing daughter Monica, who is a self-assured young woman, I would enjoy knowing that this book influenced the direction your life will take.

To all my loyal customers, friends, colleagues, and mentors, thank you for inspiring and motivating me along the difficult, but fulfilling journey that is my life.

To my incredible staff, the people who have helped keep me together through it all: Jan Fishburn, Gursewak Dhaliwal, Milagro and Yolanda Alvarado, Melchor Maldonado, Ricardo Ibarra, and the rest of our associates and food brokers who contribute to the day-to-day operation of Lulu's Dessert, thank you. To our loyal customers, your acceptance of Lulu's Dessert since its inception has motivated me to continue creating and innovating the ready-to-eat gelatin industry.

A special thank you to Sharon Freeman, Ph.D., for being my mentor and the person who opened my eyes to the possibility of writing this book. I'm also grateful to those who graciously provided inspirational words in the foreword and testimonials for this book.

I thank WBusiness Books for providing support in the development of this book. Arthur Chou, my publisher, didn't doubt there would be a strong demand for such a book. I thank Mirna Medina, for her invaluable work, dedication and complete availability during the writing of the book.

And finally, I would like to take this opportunity to thank and honor a woman who has been an inspiration to me for many years. Her name was Ana Maria Arias; she was the founder of **Latina** *Style*, "a national magazine for the contemporary Hispanic woman." Ana Maria and her husband Robert Bard, who has continued her legacy, invited me to share my story in San Diego fifteen years ago. There, I was very impressed by their energy and dedication. They traveled across the country educating Latinas in small business, the reason for the magazine. I'm honoring Ana Maria for being a role model for all Latinas, and for all her accomplishments at such a young age. Ana Maria represents the great spirit, determination, and love inherent in all Latinas, in all women.

Thank you, Robert Bard for all of the support you have provided not only to me, but to so many Latinas around the country. Thank you, *Padrino[1]:* only you understand the challenges we have had to overcome to open the doors to the next generation of Latinas.

To my readers, it is my privilege and honor that you are taking the time to read this work.

Maria de Lourdes Sobrino
Founder/CEO
Lulu's Dessert Corporation

---

[1] Padrino: godfather

# Introduction

When I first contemplated the idea of writing a book, I was in Washington, D.C., three thousand miles away from home. Dr. Sharon Freeman, President of All American Small Business Exporters Association, Inc. (AASBEA), an experienced author of many books and expert on the economies of various countries has become my mentor throughout the years. She has conducted studies on women in business in over one hundred countries and after I was part of her book *Conversations with Women Who Export,* she approached me with the suggestion of writing my own book in 2001. Never in my wildest dreams had I considered such an endeavor. Another driving factor for the development of this book came from the many conferences and speaking engagements in which I have taken part. Many people asked for advice about starting their businesses, and I realized that my story was inspirational and that I could make it instructional.

It has taken many years to bring this project to fruition, whether from lack of focus on a single subject, lack of time, or lack of knowledge about the publishing industry. Many times I felt publishing a book was an impossible dream. The more I learned from watching business women signing their books at conferences, the more I thought about putting the effort into writing my book. Once I found a subject, I made time outside of running my business to write my story. The final step was to find the right publisher. Communicating with my colleagues proved to be the best research. When I shared my desire to write a book with my friend Maria del Mar Velasco, Vice President of Learning for Entrepreneurs Organization (EO), she immediately introduced me to my publisher. I also felt it was time to showcase other successful Latina business owners like myself. They too wanted to share their stories of triumphs and tribulations, and give their insightful vision to the next generation of female entrepreneurs. We want to inspire, motivate, and give back; we all want to save people time and effort by sharing the obstacles we have overcome. It was time to write a book about Latina entrepreneurs who are making a difference.

I feel privileged to call all of the extraordinary and inspiring women in this book my friends. One of the greatest rewards I've had creating this book has been getting to better know the women as well as their businesses. Although our businesses range from food manufacturing to construction to travel to health to publishing to event marketing to the import/export of flowers, we went through very similar obstacles and have a lot in common. Our businesses are a distinct reflection of who we are. We are all thriving Latina entrepreneurs interested in sharing our stories to empower others to succeed. If we all did it, you can do it too!

All have triumphed over tremendous odds. Each one of these women is an advocate for ethics in business, delivering impressive business results that have led them to where they are today. All were gracious enough to allocate time for this project. While they have all received recognition for their achievements, most of them have not been part of a book. They found the idea very enticing and challenging. The criteria for selecting these women included primarily, that they be Latinas, whether they were immigrants like myself, or descendants of Latinos. They had to be founder of their own business, and had to still be running their business today.

There are many common threads and characteristics in the stories of these women evident within this book. You will discover many ways to approach business. Our stories provide many lessons, and present an opportunity to learn from the process we went through to find our business niche. Women were included in this book because they have achieved their dreams of becoming entrepreneurs. With this book in hand, you can become a Thriving Entrepreneur as well. These are the women who will share their stories in the following pages:

- **Maria de Lourdes Sobrino:** Founder and CEO of Lulu's Dessert Corporation, a pioneering food-manufacturing company in Anaheim, California, which revolutionized the food industry with the introduction of ready-to-eat gelatin desserts to America's grocers from my mother's recipe. I was born and raised in Mexico City.

- **Liza Roeser Atwood:** President of FiftyFlowers.com, an importer of Ecuadorian flowers to the U.S. and Farms Exports Inc., a wholesaler and distributor of flowers around the world based in Ojai, California. Liza was born in Cape Girardeau, Missouri. Her grandmother was Cuban.

- **Martha De La Torre:** Publisher of *El Clasificado,* a multi-media publication and advertising solutions company. Its Spanish-language publications are fast becoming the nation's leading platforms for reaching the Hispanic market in Southern California and beyond. Martha was born in Los Angeles to Ecuadorian parents.

- **Patricia Pliego-Stout:** President of The Alamo Travel Group, Inc., a travel-service provider with corporate offices in San Antonio, Texas. Her business has expanded to provide corporate, leisure, federal, and state travel services. Patricia was born and raised in Mexico City.

- **Olga Martinez:** President of Allright Diversified Services, a construction and engineering company specializing in federal contracting based in Fresno, California. Olga was born in the Central Valley of California to Mexican parents.

- **Carolina Jovenich:** CEO of Caroline Promotions, Inc., an event, marketing, staffing, and coordinating company based in Glendale, California. Carolina was born and raised in Buenos Aires, Argentina.

- **Theresa Alfaro Daytner:** President of Daytner Construction Group a construction management and consultant company based in Maryland. Theresa was born in Tacoma Park, Maryland of South American descent.

- **Martha E. Lugo-Aguayo:** Managing Partner/Vice President, Spectrum Benefits Group, an employee benefits and insurance company based in Woodland Hills, California. Martha was born in New York to Puerto Rican parents.

I believe people must constantly adapt to new strategies to advance in business. To improve your learning curve, study the success stories and apply what is relevant to your career. The stories of these remarkable women are inspiring and motivational. Helping people in their business and personal life is one of the most important benefits of this book.

I also wanted to provide the potential entrepreneur with solid, useful information that she can use to start her own business. In the second part of this book you will find a basic outline of the subjects I found most important in the development of my businesses:

- Chapter 9: Establishing Your Business As a Latina
- Chapter 10: Ideas for Financing
- Chapter 11: What Marketing Is all About
- Chapter 12: Branding Concepts You Should Know First
- Chapter 13: Valuable Resources for Latinas

Congratulations for taking the first step toward becoming a thriving entrepreneur!

# Section I:
# The Stories

# Chapter 1:
# Maria de Lourdes Sobrino

Founder and CEO
Lulu's Dessert Corporation
*www.lulusdessert.com, www.lulusobrino.com*

I have always had a strong entrepreneurial spirit. I think of it as *determinación*[2]—it has led me to where I am today. The road I chose has been a difficult and exciting one from my beginnings in Mexico City to my current home in Los Angeles, California. *Determinación* helped me build a multimillion dollar corporation from my tiny kitchen more than twenty-five years ago.

I come from a privileged background compared to the rest of my countrymen, as I was born into a middle-class family. However, I have never considered myself above anything or anyone. I am a hard worker, a motivated individual, a strong woman, all qualities required of entrepreneurs. Anyone who can create opportunities for herself can achieve what I have achieved. All it takes is *determinación* and a belief in oneself.

To understand where I am as a Latina entrepreneur today, it is necessary to share where I have been. This work is not an autobiography, so it will not delve into every detail of my life. It will take you through the most definitive moments, the ones that shaped me into the entrepreneur and woman I have become. My objective is that this exercise in self-description will help those who want to start or

---

[2] Spanish words will appear throughout this chapter. The literal translation for determinación is determination; synonyms include willpower, resolve, and fortitude.

continue their own business. It is not an easy road, but if I had to do it all over again, I would not change a single turn.

## Natural-Born Entrepreneur

It was natural for me to become an entrepreneur after seeing my grandparents and father have their own business. One grandfather was a lawyer and the other owned an auto shop. One of my grandmothers was a piano teacher, while the other made beautiful 1950s-style hats. My father, Arturo Sobrino Pellón was one of the best civil attorneys in Mexico City. He loved the law and was an amazing public speaker thanks to his strong personality, which I inherited. Always in a suit, he instilled the value of professionalism and appropriate presentation. He always wanted me to be a lawyer, but I had other plans.

My mother, Alicia Franco Saavedra, chose to be a traditional Mexican mother instead of continuing to work when she married my father. One talent she greatly developed as a homemaker was making gelatins. Eating gelatins is an ingrained custom in Mexican culture and she was well-known for her treats. Every time we were invited to a celebration, my mother made large, two-layered, fruit-filled gelatin desserts. Everybody loved them. The gelatin-making skills my mother taught me along with the entrepreneurial spirit my father and grandparents passed on to me would one day merge in the formation of Lulu's Dessert Corporation.

## First Foray Into Business

At fourteen years of age, after accidentally finding out about a dangerous case on which my father was working, I realized the dependency my entire family had on him. I saw a necessity, as many young Latinas do, to help my family in the immediate sense, and not necessarily wait to "become a lawyer."

Instead of going to a university, I choose to enroll in a vocational career to join the business world sooner. I received a certificate as a private accountant and executive bilingual secretary from Helena Herlihy Hall (HHH), an all-girl Catholic school in Mexico City. After graduating from HHH at the age of seventeen, I was full of energy and ready to conquer the world. Fortunately, I was lucky to get a job at IBM a day after graduation. In the information-systems department of seventeen men, I was the only woman. A few weeks after I started working at IBM, I found out they wanted to train the first woman to become a systems programmer in Latin America. My supervisor did not believe a woman would be interested in or capable of working on computers in 1969. I *was,* and after being asked about it, I told him that I would prove that "Mexican women are capable of anything." He agreed to send me, but on one condition: If I failed any of the courses, I would be removed from the program immediately.

My male coworkers, the majority of who had engineering backgrounds, thought I would not understand COBOL or perforating cards, and that I would become frustrated working at night on the IBM 1401 computer system housed in a refrigerated room. Back in the 1970s, women in Mexico were not treated as men's equals in the business world. I realized my advantage right away: They did not think of me as competition. I tried harder than they did, worked longer than they did, and learned a lot more than they did. I had something to prove, not only to them but to myself, and I did it with *determinación.* It was no easy task, but I was not going to give up. In finishing this program, I earned everyone's respect, especially that of my boss. My certificate said I was the first female "Systems Programmer" in Mexico.

Becoming the first female Systems Programmer confirmed that business, not law, was the right choice for me. I also realized I could exceed other's expectations. However, most important was the realization that I could maneuver my way through a bunch of testosterone, not only because I'm a woman, but because I'm a capable woman.

Without this experience it would have been impossible to make it through the male-driven obstacles in my career.

## The Search for a New Adventure

I was ready to move on. I was no longer passionate about the solitary work I was doing with computers; I needed to work with people. My next endeavor would be business-oriented but I was not sure what field of business I would pursue.

After a short self-financed trip to Europe I continued with my business journey. I found a job in the Groups and Conventions Department for Fiesta Palace Hotel in 1971. It was my first glimpse into public relations and the tourism industry.

At the Fiesta Palace Hotel I was trained on how to organize various events from conferences to corporate workshops and weddings. One of my successes was organizing promotional events for the Caesars Palace and Circus Circus hotels in Las Vegas. Caesars Palace was so happy with my work they offered me a job in Las Vegas three months before my wedding. I decided against it and instead, spent time organizing my wedding in Mexico. I enjoyed my job at the Fiesta Palace Hotel very much thanks to the experiences I had and the people I met, however, it was not challenging enough. My entrepreneurial spirit did not allow me to work for someone else for long.

## My First Business

My first business was called *La Florería Inglesa*[3]. I really enjoyed flowers and because I was already purchasing flowers wholesale for the events I organized, it made sense to start a business within the same industry. With personal savings and no business plan but a lot of confidence, I started in 1972. This is something I recommend to burgeoning entrepreneurs so they don't lose income: Start a new venture *on the side* first; keep your day job.

---

[3] *La Florería Inglesa:* The English Flower Shop

I asked my mother to help with the flower shop while continuing my job at the Fiesta Palace Hotel. Since the business began to flourish, I opened a second flower shop at the Hotel Del Prado three years later.

While still at the Fiesta Palace Hotel, I started organizing events at other venues around the country. That is how my second business, Turismo Copsa was born that same year, 1975. I didn't know it at the time but I was creating the first company specializing in organizing groups, conventions, and events for various companies throughout Mexico. I hired six employees and added a Travel Groups Division months later, sending Mexican tourists to Las Vegas, Los Angeles, and San Francisco.

My business was doing very well; it was so successful that an international office was needed to keep up with the demand of my services. This is where I must point out that my plight to come to the United States in 1982 was different than that of most other Latino immigrants. I had the means to hire an attorney to help me incorporate and start my third business, Mexico and Westside Connections, Inc.

Even though the decision to expand to the U.S. was made primarily because of business growth, there was a personal underlying reason. The promise of a new life with my husband and five-year-old daughter was very enticing. Also, coming to the United Sates would fulfill one of my greatest dreams: Disneyland. Who knew that one day I was going to promote and bring Mexican tourism to Disneyland?

## Journey to the U.S.

You have to keep in mind that at that time, Mexico's border was not as open for trade as it is now. Importing clothes, toys, food, or other things was difficult. This was something I did not understand when I was younger, and even when I started Turismo Copsa. My curiosity for doing business in America was always present. It was difficult to understand why my world was limited to a border.

Traveling beyond that border gave me the opportunity to work in the country I had always wanted to visit, and to open the border to tourism.

While I know that I was not the first and only person to open the border for business between the two countries, it felt very rewarding to start building bridges. Fortunately, I was able to obtain my immigration documents as an investor. I got an L-1 Visa to work in Mexico and Westside Connections, Inc., exclusively. It was not a difficult process then because I arrived as an investor transferred by my Mexican company. However, to have that paperwork for my future endeavors was very useful.

Before I left, I first had to tell my parents that I wanted to leave Mexico and temporarily move to the U.S. My family in Mexico thought I would be back in a few months; no one considered that I would oneday live in the United States. I left my Turismo Copsa office in Mexico City in operation in 1982 and sold my flower shops. The hardest part for me was leaving my family who I love dearly.

The words "immigrant," "minority," and "Latina" were not part of my vocabulary before coming to America. It is important to understand that with a huge population, Mexico is a large country with rural and metropolitan areas. I come from Mexico City, the capital, with around twenty-five million people. Most Mexican immigrants in America do not come from Mexico City; rather, they come from smaller rural areas of Mexico.

It was a real shock to be called a minority because I came from a big homogenous city. Today I am proud to be called a Latina because I see it is an advantage. I try to take advantage of whatever privileges are associated with being a woman-owned firm or a Hispanic-owned firm. Latina or Hispanic, both of these labels are positive and I am proud to be called either one.

I opened my first Mexico and Westside Connections, Inc. office on Century Boulevard across the street from LAX, but a few months later something happened that changed my plans, my future, and ultimately, my life.

## Life Decided by the *Peso*

I watched in horror as the value of Mexican pesos plunged against the U.S. dollar in 1982. One day the peso was worth a good amount, and the next day, it was worth almost nothing. This horrible devaluation killed my travel business. It made my services prohibitively expensive for a predominantly Mexican clientele. The country plunged into chaos. Nothing was the same since the economy had suffered so terribly. My business took a dive and worse yet, my going back to Mexico was not the best idea.

I was scared of the economic and political situation in Mexico. I heard of atrocities occurring there because people needed goods and services and suddenly the money they had was worth almost nothing. Fear was ever present and I did not want to expose my family or myself to the dangers of such uncertainty. On top of that, my husband did not want to stay in U.S. Reluctantly, he agreed to stay for a couple of years because of the turmoil going on in my country.

I was determined to hold on to my travel business. I tried to develop it by offering tourism from the U.S. to Mexico, but I failed miserably. To develop any kind of business, a network is needed, whether it be to generate customers or for support and idea generation. I did not have that.

My husband and daughter were the only support system I had. No colleagues or business partners were around to turn to. One of the hardest things for an immigrant was not knowing anyone. Ultimately, I had to stop trying to send tourism to Mexico. Some people could not even afford food; next to nobody could afford to travel.

With no business to keep me here, my parents, relatives, and husband began pressuring me to return to Mexico. I felt cornered, depressed, and above all, desperate. After all the hard work I had put into coming to the United States, my efforts were going to be tossed away. This was very emotionally and physically draining.

To top it all off, the food here was different, and having to give up a more comfortable lifestyle was difficult. The language barrier made it difficult too. Everything was strange to me because it was in English; *estaba sola*[4].

Loneliness was tearing me apart. Suddenly, I doubted myself and my decisions. I asked myself, "why are you doing this?"

It took some courage, but I analyzed my situation and found that my entrepreneurial spirit reminded me of *determinación*. This was the beginning of the adventure that has defined me as a Latina entrepreneur, the adventure of Lulu's Dessert.

## The Beginning of Lulu's Dessert

One day I was looking for the traditional Mexican dessert that is a staple in my native Mexico, ready-to-eat gelatins. I couldn't find them in stores in Redondo Beach, where I was living. I started doing research by visiting grocery stores in my area but could not find any. Since my mother taught me how to make the gelatin dessert, I would go to Tijuana to buy ingredients and make gelatins from scratch. They were delicious, just like I remembered. It was great because it allowed me to teach my daughter how to make the *gelatinas*[5] I loved so much. We spent countless hours in the kitchen working on perfecting our three-colored, layered masterpieces. Those hours were wonderful; they form part of my fondest memories as a mother and entrepreneur.

After sharing gelatin samples with my neighbors and others, I began receiving positive feedback. Most of them had never seen gelatin made in different shaped molds before. They had only been exposed to the powder mix in a box from brands like JELL-O and Royal.

All the people with whom I shared my *gelatina* loved it and thought I could make a business selling it. I didn't know what I was

---

[4] *Estaba sola:* I was alone
[5] *gelatinas:* gelatins

getting myself into; however, the entrepreneur inside me was curious and ecstatic. I had finally found my niche. I had a winner! I found something about which I was passionate. I cannot emphasize enough the importance of passion when it comes to starting your own business. If you have passion, you will be able to stand up to anything that gets in your way. Passion gives you energy; it gives you hope; it triggers *determinación*.

I started looking for information on the food industry. The Health and Human Services Department required that I open a legal establishment out of my home if I wanted to sell my product to the public. My lawyer recommended that instead of opening another corporation, I create a DBA (Doing Business As) and add it to the business that brought me to the U.S., Mexico, and Westside Connections Inc. That is how my fourth business, Lulu's Dessert Factory, was founded in 1982.

Looking back, I realize what a large, blind risk I took. Food manufacturing required an exponentially larger capital investment than any of my previous businesses. I began with a $50,000 cash investment, and later added the sale of two real-estate properties as needed. This was how Lulu's Dessert began.

## Branding

Brand names summon a clear image in our minds. Companies spend millions of advertising dollars each year to promote brands, but I never had that kind of budget. Instead I needed to develop a catchy name. A name was needed to get my business up and running, so I went next door to my neighbor's and brainstormed. About a hundred different names were suggested, and then I told him about my nickname, Lulu. He immediately suggested I use it.

That idea was not appealing as I was very shy. Naming the company after myself seemed too boastful. In my country, one does not promote their products with their names. But I soon realized that, in America, it was a widespread and typical practice. It did not take long to convince me. We came up with the simple, but self-descriptive name that has carried my product throughout the years, "Lulu's Dessert Factory" (which has since become a Corporation). From that point forward, my brand has been myself. I get out there and put my face on Lulu's Dessert; we are one and the same, inseparable. In lieu of a big advertising budget, I have played an instrumental role in raising my profile and keeping my story in front of my consumers to create brand loyalty.

The first thing that comes to the mind of a Latino entrepreneur is a *tiendita*[6], so I opened a gelatin store that was 700 square feet in Torrance, California. My rent was $400.00 a month. I had to exchange my pesos for dollars, and found, unfortunately, that many pesos became very few dollars. Thankfully, it was enough to open my little store. It was a small Hispanic-style eatery for which I bought all new fixtures and equipment. I was very proud of this new accomplishment. There, I sold Mexican style sandwiches as well as coffee, juices, cookies, cake-sized gelatins, individual-figurine gelatins on a *papelito*[7], and other desserts. All of these products were prepared by me the night before. This still required a weekly trip to Tijuana to buy my ingredients, as I did not know where to find them around my neighborhood.

Grand Opening of My *Tiendita* in Torrance, California

---

[6] tiendita: small retail store
[7] papelito: small paper

Unfortunately, nobody understood my products and I was not selling enough. After three months I was very tired, opening the *tiendita* from 8 a.m. to 9 p.m., Monday through Saturday. It was so tiring that I was ready to give up and close the store.

## From *Tienda* to Factory

Instead of giving up, I decided to convert my *tiendita* into a small factory. If customers couldn't find me, I needed to find customers. My product had to be put into retail stores and I needed to find a way to do just that. That is when I put the gelatin in a single-portion clear cup, designed my label, and began looking for customers. Because I was introducing a traditional Mexican dessert, I needed to find first-generation Mexicans who would understand the cultural and even emotional value—the nostalgia—of gelatin. The Mexican community in Los Angeles concentrated itself in various sections of the city. Redondo Beach, where I settled, was not one of those places.

I realized there were also a lot of second-generation Mexicans who would be interested in a cultural-food desert, such as my gelatin. There were a lot of Latinos in places like Wilmington, Carson, and Long Beach, and I set out to find them. My tactic was to pursue mom-and-pop stores in those cities. At first, the store owners laughed at my product. They didn't understand the concept because I didn't have any competition. They asked why people would buy the gelatin if they could easily make it at home. After convincing them of the convenience of the ready-to-eat product, I asked their permission to leave it at the store on a consignment basis at no risk to them. I knew if they let me put the gelatin in their refrigerator, they would see that the deserts could be sold.

## *Jarrita* in Hand

One day I delivered to a store in the morning and by late afternoon I received a phone call. The owner said, " *Señora*[8], please come back; your *gelatinas* are sold out and we need more." This phone call

---

[8] *Señora: ma'am*

motivated me. I still hold those difficult times close to my heart. It is important to remember that fundamentally, the business started with only basic ingredients combined with *determinación*. I started by producing three hundred cups a day. Each gelatin had three layers, so I actually had to fill the cups 900 times, armed only with my *jarrita*[9], my apron, and my recipe book. Those objects are now part of the *Latinas: The Spirit of California* exhibit at the California Museum for History, "Women and the Arts" in Sacramento.

This business was an experiment for my husband, my daughter and for me. It was an adventure for all of us to a certain point, because we had not yet decided that we were going to live in this country permanently. My family in Mexico was confused and amused by my entrepreneurial pursuits. They couldn't comprehend that I was making a living selling a dessert. They laughed because they pictured my business as a pushcart on the streets of downtown Los Angeles. My father was ready to see me return as a big failure and I did not want to give him the pleasure of saying, *"te lo dije, hija*[10]." I worked very hard to make it in America; my *determinación* was incredibly strong.

## Off to a Running Start

Two months later representatives from The Boys Markets were visiting mom-and-pop stores, trying to understand what Mexicans ate and bought. Remember that twenty-five years ago, only tortillas and salsas were found in supermarkets. The reps found my products and contacted me through a food broker. They explained the job of a broker and we started doing business together on a commission basis. When they gave me an order for one thousand cases I said to them, "I do not think it is going to be possible to produce one thousand cases. Do you know how much work that is?" So I had a good problem: *growth*. I needed a plan for financing, production, shipping, and giving terms to my customers. Having no credit with a bank, I decided to invest the last of the savings I brought from

[9] *jarrita:* little jar; pitcher
[10] *Te lo dije hija:* I told you so, daughter

Mexico to take the company to the next level. I was very excited about my adventure. It was now time to take a big leap; consignment was no longer an option because I had started a full-fledged business.

By 1984 I had moved from the little store in Torrance to an industrial building in Gardena. The building had been an auto body shop. After purchasing it, I converted it into a small food-manufacturing plant. There, I felt more like an industrial manufacturer. I began hiring employees, finding suppliers, inventing and designing a filler system, and buying more equipment. I spent at least five difficult years working on a formula that had a sixty-day shelf life. I continued the development of a full line of gelatins in different sizes. All of them are favorites of mine, but my mother's favorites were, and still are, the creamy ones.

## The Power of Free

To promote my products, I gave away free samples in supermarkets. This rudimentary method was the only form of marketing I knew of, but it gave me the opportunity to receive feedback from customers. This is what marketing companies call "focus groups"; but I did it informally, and most critically, personally. The lesson here is that you have to get to know your consumers. Being amicable and responsive is incredibly important. Each contact you make is a potential marketer for your product, and combined with word-of-mouth advertising from these consumers, the markets for your products can increase exponentially.

Another well-learned lesson is that the Hispanic community is fiercely loyal. However, it takes a lot to be able to capture its loyalty. A product has to be of great quality, affordable, and innovative in order to capture our attention. I am glad I learned that early on.

To expand the business I decided to process other food products in my plant. These included pickled carrots, coated soy peanuts, and liquid vanilla. However, when my customers complained about my gelatins tasting like *chile*, I investigated and found that gelatin is like a sponge; it absorbs everything in the air. Little by little, I discontinued the other lines. The lesson here is to *stay focused on what you are doing to be the best in one category.*

## Ready-to-Eat

Lulu's Dessert Corporation has been credited with being the first company to introduce the category of ready-to-eat gelatin dessert in individual portion sizes to the supermarkets of America. It took my major competitor, Kraft Food's Jell-O, eleven years to catch up to where I began in offering a similar product and when they did catch on, they jumped in with everything they had. They hired actor Bill Cosby to promote their gelatin in ready-to-eat individual portions. I thought I was going to disappear, but thanks to the advertisements, Bill Cosby was educating the consumer about ready-to-eat gelatin. My sales started increasing, and the category expanded.

## Staying Connected With People Outside

It is important to stay in touch with people outside your work environment to bring in fresh ideas. In those days I couldn't find a network of business people with whom to communicate. There was no Internet, nor was I aware of any conferences to attend. I decided to take night classes on different subjects at the local community college. This was a welcome distraction from the hard work of running a company and allowed me to think outside the business.

## "Million-Dollar Baby"

Financially speaking, I didn't have a salary for about three years since I let the company function with its own profits. One day my bank mentioned that I could apply for a Small Business Administration (SBA) loan. When I asked what the loan was, the banker explained that it is a low-interest loan that the government guarantees—a program to help businesses. I prepared a business plan with a consultant for the first time in my life, and applied. In 1989, I received a 504 SBA loan of close to one million dollars that gave me the ability to expand and buy a larger building. This allowed me to move Lulu's to the next level; this time it was a 15,000-square-foot plant in Huntington Beach, California.

## Personal Disappointments

Sometimes to make things happen in business, family time and relationships suffer. It is not that one prefers the business to family; it is simply that one does not see this occurring until it happens. Unfortunately, my personal life was not going well. I did not have my then-husband's support; instead, he made me believe that I didn't have the right to be successful. The relationship was deteriorating after many years of struggle. Moreover, I painfully lost legal custody of my daughter Lourdes. After many years of fighting in court for her custody, I had to let her go based on her wishes. More traumatic to me was the fact that I had lost her emotionally.

I was extremely vulnerable and in my attempt to move on, I entered a new relationship in which I had my second daughter, Monica. After dealing with another man who didn't accept me as an independent woman, but before getting into more trouble, I left him.

I continued to focus on the company. Enthusiastic about my loan and the growth of my sales, I was able to dedicate more energy and thus recouped some lost time. Obtaining my SBA loan was difficult, as was moving into my new plant in Huntington Beach in Orange County, California. Finally, in 1989, I had a new beginning.

Moving to the Huntington Beach plant took much more time than I had anticipated. There were about nine months' worth of permits to remodel the building and work with the city. I was suffering financially since I was operating the Huntington Beach and the Gardena plant at the same time. I had a budget but it was not enough and the money ran out before I could finish improvements on the building. I had to look at new financing and take risks working with new banks on different types of loans and leases. While I was in this process and working with one of my vendors, I realized the plant was too big to produce only gelatin desserts. So there I went again: I created a new company, this time with a 50/50 partner.

## Fancy Fruit Corporation

In 1990, my new partner and I put our strengths together and sealed this new partnership with a simple handshake. I knew how to make *gelatinas,* while my partner knew how to make *paletas[11]*. This was the start of my fifth business: Fancy Fruit Corporation. This time around, I had no initial capital, but I did have more experience. By now, I understood the American way of living with debt and paying interest. There was a time when there were more than twenty loans financing both Lulu's Dessert and Fancy Fruit. This came from a strong desire to diversify to a new food category. There was excitement in creating another new company from nothing. We built our own equipment in house and were producing *gelatinas* and *paletas* in the same production room. It wasn't long before we had growth problems for both companies.

Fancy Fruit provided me with a lot of knowledge about a different division of the food industry. After all, one was a frozen, and the other was a refrigerated product. Again, I didn't have any idea what I was doing but I was learning and my partner, with his engineering background, was helping me to improve the machinery for Lulu's. I did very brief research on the marketing side.

Given that *paletas* are also a very well-known product in the Mexican community, I thought everything was going to work out, and that we would be able to combine Lulu's Dessert and Fancy

---

[11] *paletas:* ice cream bars

Fruit sales. A year into working with both products, I realized they were completely different worlds. I learned the deli buyer is different from the frozen-food buyer. We needed two different types of distribution channels, and thus different sales departments, different distribution trucks, and so forth.

## Costly Exporting

My export experience began with my shipping Fancy Fruit bars around the world far too soon. I was not prepared to go to that level yet. One day we received a call from a customer who wanted to export our fruit bars to England. He came to the U.S. and bought one in a store. He found he liked it and wanted to export it to the UK. We were very excited when he visited us to order the first truckload. We asked him for payment in advance. The second truck was on consignment basis, and it took him six months to pay. The third truck took him a year to pay. In conclusion, we didn't know that we could request a *Letter of Credit* to guarantee the sale. Ultimately, the same scenario played out in Chile, Australia, New Zealand, and Puerto Rico among others.

There came a point when we could not afford to put out all the receivables. The company continued producing with the financial support received from Lulu's Dessert. My partner and I traveled to all these countries trying to collect our money and found out that it is very difficult to legally collect because each country has its own laws. Once goods are out of the U.S., you lose control. We needed to hire legal advice in each country, and found it to be very costly. Years later, I learned that the U.S. Commercial Service from the Department of Commerce, through the information they provide, could have saved us from making the mistakes we made. At the same time, the U.S. Export-Import Bank could have provided financing if we had known about it. The lesson learned through my impulsiveness was that there is a lot of free and valuable information available, but you have to do your research.

## Complications

By mid 1992 so many difficulties had occurred that I was ready to give up and close my business. On top of everything, my father passed away from diabetes complications. As I sunk into a deep depression, other things started falling apart. We were exporting *paletas* around the world and had a large amount of receivables that we could not collect. I was trying very hard to keep both companies going but it did not look promising.

Due to the 1992 L.A. riots that year, I lost the Gardena plant. People burned many properties in the area and nobody wanted to buy it. I was forced to return the building to its previous owners. Compounding my problems, I lost my home in Torrance since the recession in the early 1990s had made interest rates skyrocket. My company was behind on taxes and the IRS was ready to close my doors if I didn't pay up. I borrowed money from my parents, and my brother Arturo also helped me keep going, but the debt was too big this time.

I prayed to God, asking Him for help. I was desperate, but Monica, my youngest daughter, gave me the strength to continue. Giving up was not an option. Fortunately, my employees also gave me the energy to go back and fight for the companies. One day while looking at the conveyors, I realized that thousands of customers depended on our products. I couldn't fail the customers who had supported and been loyal to Lulu's for so many years. Also, there were many people that depended upon my decisions: suppliers, banks, brokers, distributors, and especially my employees. I had to believe in myself and thus I reverted to my *determinación*.

I moved into a small apartment close to the plant to grieve the loss of my father and to figure out what I should do. That gave me some time to resolve my problems one by one. I sought support and started talking to mentors who helped me better understand the business and the different options I had, and helped me learn from my mistakes. Thanks to these experiences, I became a stronger woman. I continued to develop more desserts using common sense and studying my customer's needs.

## How I Developed Our Best-Selling Item

Creating my best-selling item—the twelve-pack of assorted, single-color gelatins—came from a realization I had while shopping at a grocery store. I saw a customer buying several cups of Lulu's Dessert. She put them all in her arms; then she put them in her shopping cart and walked back to the produce department to get a plastic bag in which to place her gelatins. That is when it occurred to me to put together a family pack; it was my job to accommodate her needs.

The next day, I started experimenting with a piece of cardboard and the cups of gelatin. I placed twelve cups on the cardboard, shrink-wrapped them, put a label on them, and presto! The twelve-pack was born. We introduced it to the market for testing and to this day, it is the number-one-selling item in the company. This is an example of how important it is to understand your consumers' needs, and immediately act on your findings.

As soon as the product hit the shelves, competitors imitated the idea. When a company or a product is successful, it always runs the risk of being imitated. However, Lulu's Dessert has always been the innovator in the gelatin category, and no one will ever take that away from me. There are certain things that cannot be patented, but for those that can be, make sure you consult a lawyer to guide you through the trademarking steps.

## Real Estate: A New Business

Lulu's Dessert needed to expand again and this time I wanted to build a plant. Since I was becoming familiar with buying and leasing buildings, I decided to do it myself That is how my sixth business, Arroyo Vista was born in 1997. Arroyo Vista was created for the purpose of building a state-of-the-art plant for Lulu's Dessert. I bought four acres of land in Rancho Santa Margarita in Orange County and began the planning and legal processes. It took me about two and one-half years to obtain permits and everything else necessary for construction. All this time, the Huntington Beach plant was in operation.

We were ready to start construction on a Friday, when I received a phone call from one of my suppliers on Tuesday of the same week. He convinced me to visit a plant that was going on sale in the city of Vernon. I fell in love with the plant in Vernon as soon as I saw it. A life-changing decision had to be made between continuing the construction in Rancho Santa Margarita or taking the available plant. I could not sleep that night and the next day, I met with the construction team and analyzed the Vernon-plant offer.

Even after Baskin Robbins (the owners of the property) learned that I was very interested but I was not financially prepared, they accepted my position and decided to finance me. I signed to buy a multi-million-dollar property for Lulu's Dessert Corporation and Fancy Fruit, which I had fully acquired a year earlier. I was very scared, but thrilled! After all the effort that went into the new plant project, I had to take my losses and start manufacturing at a larger scale as soon as possible.

## With Risks Come Rewards

As I look back, it is hard to believe the number of risks that I took for my business, starting with the $400 in rent I paid in 1982 for my *tiendita*. I then spent thousands of dollars for the Gardena plant, and then millions for the Vernon plant. This is how small businesses contribute to the U.S. economy. As far as the construction project with Arroyo Vista, I made a profit when the land was sold, but took my losses of about a million dollars when the project was never built.

The plan to move again in 2000 to Vernon included making a decision about whether or not I should move Fancy Fruit, which had been in operation for ten years at that point. However, lack of capital was once again an obstacle. Lulu's Dessert was my priority so I decided to stop manufacturing with Fancy Fruit. Being an entrepreneur involves making difficult decisions that you may not personally want to make, but are financially forced into.

Vernon Plant in 2000

Another lesson to learn from this is that you can always look to outside investors to keep your company afloat. Back then my way of looking at business did not allow me to see this because I was overwhelmed. The company shouldn't have closed and at this point it would have been operating in the Huntington Beach plant if I had had financing.

I was under a lot of pressure to increase production since many customers were waiting while I was busy building plants. Finally, we moved to the 64,000–square-foot Vernon plant and organized a grand opening for our customers, suppliers, friends, and the community. I was very proud. At last, my staff was going to have the space they deserved, the parking, a number of bathrooms, a lunchroom, a lab for quality control and a large warehouse to store materials and refrigerate product. It had everything we needed; it was the state-of-the-art plant that I'd always dreamed of owning.

During the time I spent working on the new plant, I did not pay attention to the competition. They started copying all of my products and taking away some of my customers. It was time to get back to what I do best, innovating and branding.

## The Media

According to the U.S. Census Bureau, by 2020, there will be more than 59 million people of Hispanic origin living in the United States, and by 2050, there will be 100 million. According to the Center for Women's Business Research, "More than a third . . . of firms majority owned by women of color are majority owned by Hispanic/Latina women." As a result, more attention was being placed on Latinos by the media, and I eventually used that to my advantage.

In 1998, the media began paying attention to me. After I'd gone unnoticed for years, *The Orange County Register* called one day to request an interview that was published soon after. From that point on, it snowballed and I could not stop it. Since then, I have been on numerous covers, featured in countless articles. and made many television appearances.

It is a great time in American history to be Latino. Slowly, I have become engaged in the process of building the Lulu's Dessert brand. As a result, I spend every moment working on Lulu's Dessert, whether at the factory or at networking affairs and special events outside the office. I have been recognized with many awards and am involved in numerous boards and community events, thanks in part to media coverage. All of these things have been instrumental for my company and my self-improvement.

## Awards

In 1998 the chairman of the Latin Business Association (LBA), Hector Barreto, awarded me the LBA "Woman of the Year Award." This award opened the door of the Los Angeles business community for me. Then I received the Avon Award in New York in 1999 where I was treated like a queen. The event was held at the Waldorf Astoria. My daughter and my mother, Alicia, along with the rest of my family and friends—a total of thirty—five people-came to New York to celebrate this accomplishment with me. I was in heaven and living one of the best moments of my life.

That was where I gave my first speech as a Latina entrepreneur; I was so nervous but at the same time, proud of being at the podium. My family later asked why I was recognized since I was just a business owner. In Mexico, there is only recognition for very high government officials or scientists. I explained that because America's economy moves constantly, the country is good at motivating the small businesses and creating jobs and wealth.

I have great memories of every award received and conference attended. I have been motivated by and learned so much from other entrepreneurs and their stories. We all go through a similar process and learn from each other. This was when national coverage of my story and company was in full effect. For example, articles were written about me in *USA Today, The Wall Street Journal,* and *The Washington Post.* There was also a piece on CNN in Spanish and an interview by Peter Jennings of ABC News. Many articles have been particularly important in raising my profile among Spanish speakers in the U.S. and throughout Latin America. One of them appeared in *La Opinión.*

My good friend Robert Bard, publisher of *Latina Style* magazine, wrote an article entitled "How Sweet It Is: The Creation of a Dessert Empire" about my story and put me on the front cover of his magazine in 2002. I felt very honored when I saw my picture on the front cover of the most important magazine for Latinas. This article has become part of the portfolio I send to my customers.

I was also lucky enough to attend a global conference in Bermuda for Leading Women Entrepreneurs of the World where I met highly successful women from all over the globe. It was news to me that women could own private jets! I felt surrounded by powerful women that are contributing so much to the world. They had businesses much larger than mine but we all had the ability to embrace risk, and *determinación.*

Receiving awards not only increases your profile as a business owner, but also helps your company's credibility, and draws even more media exposure. I have been fortunate to receive countless awards, many of which I will not mention here, but that have brought me joy and pride.

## Political Networking

Since 1999 I have been invited to a number of events in Washington, D.C. Aida Alvarez, former SBA administrator, invited me to give testimony of my company and the SBA loan I received. This gave me the understanding of the power of networking, as well as a glimpse into how the government works with businesses. I have been to the state department with Secretary of State Colin Powel, visited former Treasurer Rosario Marin, and have met senators and congresswomen. All of that gave me an understanding of the political world, and led to the opportunity to visit the White House. It is important for small-business owners to understand how they can benefit from our political system.

In 2002 I got a call from the White House asking me to represent small business in America at the Economic Forum at Bailey University in Waco, Texas. I prepared a list of suggestions so the government could better understand the needs of a small business. For example, access to capital, worker's compensation, insurance, and taxes. Access to very important people is a very valuable asset to anyone, especially small-business owners. I sat next to prominent political figures; one of them was Vice President Dick Cheney. One of the best moments was being introduced by Hector Barreto, SBA Administrator, to President George W. Bush who spoke to me in Spanish and told me his favorite Lulu's Dessert was my flan. The next day, to my surprise, my photo appeared in *The Washington Post.*

# Manufacturing

The most frequent question from people interested in producing food products involves manufacturing. Following is the list that you must be prepared to have at least a basic knowledge of, if going into the food manufacturing industry: Health Department regulations and inspections, Food and Drug Administration (FDA), Occupational Safety and Health Administration (OSHA), product development, food technology, quality control, purchasing costs, designing equipment, maintenance, refrigeration, government relations, trucking, financing, marketing, branding, sales, distribution at all levels, merchandizing, human resources, legal, accounting, construction, and public relations.

Twenty-five years ago, I did not have a clue about the complexity of food manufacturing. I also did not have a background in food processing. I had to teach myself and at the same time, hire the right people to take care of the different departments. As a consequence, I made some very costly mistakes but also learned crucial aspects of the business.

I did not consider outsourcing until I needed to become more competitive and cost-effective. Due to the constantly increasing cost of operations in California and higher costs in fuel, I had to be creative and find a way to continue in business without moving out of California. I began researching food companies that were successfully outsourcing nationwide. This business model appeared more enticing. The most important aspect of outsourcing is to have complete commitment from both parties so that both may benefit. For many years, I thought my value was in controlling everything: manufacturing, distribution, marketing, and sales. But one of the benefits of outsourcing is the ability to focus on what you do best, in my case, it was marketing, sales, and distribution of Lulu's Dessert. Therefore, I decided to give outsourcing a try. I sold sell the plant and negotiated to stay in the same building in 2004.

Now I am able to negotiate for the best price among competing bidders around the country. I now have the opportunity to avoid the long-term investment that manufacturing requires. My recommendation to those interested in food processing of items such as salsas, juices, candies, or family recipes, is to start the way I did, by making a small investment to test the market. Then looking for a company that has similar ingredients and equipment to what you want to produce. Keep in mind that you need a certain volume to guarantee the co-packer, and you probably have to invest in your own packaging at the beginning. This is less complicated than opening your own manufacturing plant.

In order to protect yourself and your product, you should hire an attorney to prepare a nondisclosure agreement as well as the details of the contract. You will avoid a lot of headaches and investment by concentrating on what you do best. However, this does not mean you should close the doors completely on manufacturing.

After outsourcing the manufacturing, we moved the corporate offices out of the plant and started focusing on the vision, marketing, product development, and distribution of our products. Now my new strategy is to leverage the brand and build strategic alliances with new partners to take Lulu's Dessert to the next level.

### *Determinación* Pays Off

If I had to go back thirty-five years and do this again, I would do it exactly the same way. Lulu's began with a little help from sugar, water, fruit, passion, and the desire to fulfill a dream. I never thought that this dream would become my life. It has been more than an adventure to go from helping my mother make her gelatin in Mexico to employing Mexicans (95% of all my employees) to make gelatins in the U.S.

Now that I am more open-minded, my story as a successful Latina is not over yet. I am in the process of making historic decisions for my company and myself. I would like to see my daughter Monica continue with the same *determinación*. My desire is that she, too, will fulfill her American dream, whatever it turns out to be.

As I am finishing this book, I am traveling with the Mayor of Los Angeles, Antonio Villaraigosa, as part of his delegation to Mexico

City. This historic trip highlights for me the privilege of being both Mexican and American. Looking toward the future, the process I began when I first arrived in the United States of building bridges with my businesses is now more resonant than ever as the world becomes more connected.

## Advice

To share my story with the younger generation of would-be entrepreneurs gives me great satisfaction. When I was starting out, I was entirely on my own. I did not have any role models or anyone to whom I could go for advice and as a result, I made a lot of avoidable mistakes.

I advise you to maintain a balanced life. Be sure to have a social, personal, and spiritual life, and not dedicate all your time to work. This may be difficult at times, but will positively impact your business in the long run.

Seek support when needed. Those who are afraid to ask spend more time and resources to find the answer. Learn as much as you can and set goals based on what you learn. Many go to conferences or read and do not follow that up with action. Find a mentor; having someone with experience to see things objectively is invaluable.

Stay true to your roots. I made it a point throughout my career to keep my Mexican ties, and even get involved in Mexico's economy and social programs. After all, my products are Mexican desserts and I am simply extending that tradition to the United States.

After thirty five years of being an entrepreneur, I still don't know it all; I learn something new everyday. I am open to new ways of doing business and I would like to take Lulu's Dessert to the next level. My story is far from over; I look forward to sharing more with you in the future.

Be persistent. **Have *determinacion.***

# Chapter 2:

# Liza Roeser Atwood

President
FiftyFlowers.com
*www.FiftyFlowers.com*
Farm Exports
*www.sassyflowers.com*

Liza Roeser Atwood was born in Cape Girardeau, Missouri, and spent most of her childhood in Dallas, Texas. Liza grew up in a bilingual and bicultural household since her grandmother was Cuban. Her family hired a Spanish-speaking caretaker to look after her and her siblings while both of her parents worked as educators. Spanish was Liza's first language prior to entering school. Once in school, English predominated and Spanish was pushed to the remote parts of her memory, but the roots had been planted.

## A Life Defined by Peace

In 1993, while attending Texas A&M for a Bachelor of Science in Tourism and Marketing, Liza organized a job fair at the university. One of the speakers at the fair was a Peace Corps representative. Due to Liza's love of helping people, she sat in on the presentation. Liza had always wanted to go to Africa, so she thought she could use the Peace Corps as the vehicle for this dream. "The Peace Corps traces its roots and mission to 1960, when then Senator John F. Kennedy challenged students at the University of Michigan to serve their country in the cause of peace by living and working in developing countries. From that inspiration grew an agency of the federal government devoted to world peace and friendship."[12] However, fate had a different destination in mind for Liza. She was assigned to Ecuador for two years instead, with only remnants of very basic Spanish from childhood still in her memory.

Following her two years of service, she stayed in Ecuador and found a job within the international flower industry. She says, "The flower industry found me—I happened to be in the right place at the right time." The day after she finished her commitment with the Peace Corps, she was hired to work with one of the largest flower farms and shipping companies in Ecuador as a Marketing and Sales Representative. As a biculturally educated person, Liza was an asset. Also, as the flower industry is one of Ecuador's top industries, the pay was attractive. Liza went from earning $20 per month in the Peace Corps to $2,000 with her new employer.

### The Roots of a New Business

Eager to learn, Liza took every feasible opportunity to educate herself about her new field. However, the flower industry is male-dominated. She says, "In general, women were disrespected and not taken seriously on a professional level." By 1997, she found herself very unhappy. Liza then began applying for new jobs but feared working in similar environments. As a result, she had two choices: On one hand, she could move back to the United States where she was sure she could find a comfortable job based on her international work experience. The U.S. professional world is vast, and can be quite daunting. Equally intimidating was her second option: to remain in Ecuador and start her own flower company. Liza was certain she was equipped with the professional experience to start her first business.

Liza was apprehensive about the risks involved in starting her own business. Creating your own enterprise requires that you break

---

[12] From www.peacecrops.org

away from the conventional lifestyle and have courage. Liza states, "I knew I had a great idea but finding the bravery to proceed was challenging. Being an employee of a company offers stability; each month you get a fixed salary with all the benefits, insurance, taxes paid, retirement plans, and so on. Starting your own business requires a lot of research and time. As the founder, not only do you have to be in charge of all departments, but you must also have the knowledge to manage these departments."

However, she was tired of the mistreatment and misguidance she had experienced at the hand of former coworkers. Liza knew she had the ability to lead people and form a great company. Not only did she want to create a successful business, but also a pleasant work environment. An additional motivation was the freedom to balance work, play, and family. In order to do this, Liza surrounded herself with Ecuadorian women who were looking for harmony, many of whom did not understand that this balance could be achieved. Liza opened a small international flower business in 1997.

Liza had been working at the farm level for three years. Although three years may not seem like much, Liza spent that time working hard, dedicated to her job. Sometimes that involved starting the day at 5:15 a.m., working until 10:00 p.m., and spending the night at a nearby bed and breakfast to get up early the next day to be at the office. After three years of working for different farms in Ecuador and Colombia, Liza knew the industry in depth.

## Cultivating Relationships

Due to the strong relationships she had been cultivating through her marketing job and the good reputation Liza had built with the farm owners, she was able to start her business. At this point, Liza had no start-up capital. She took the risk of asking for products based only on her word. Liza began representing certain farmers exclusively on a consignment basis. The result was Farm Exports. Liza had only one employee and a part-time accountant. The business was self-financed from the beginning, and to this day, the profits are reinvested in the company. Liza did not have a business plan when she started her company; she started out small, maintaining reasonable and attainable goals, and believing in herself.

## A Business in Bloom

Farm Exports has continued to grow. The first business's name was "Farm Fresh Flowers Export," which the Ecuadorian government assigned to the company. Legally in Ecuador, you cannot name your own business, but rather a name has to be approved. It took three rounds of submissions for the Ecuadorian Government to approve the name (even though misspelled) "Farmfresh Flowers Exports." In 1998 Liza formed "Farm Fresh Exports," officially doing business as "Farm Exports," a U.S. incorporated business. Farm Exports sells flowers directly from the farms to flower wholesalers around the world and promotes SASSY flowers, which are produced by their partner farms—smaller boutique farms focusing on producing top-quality, consistent, distinctive flowers. Even though today 95% of the business trade is conducted with U.S. companies, at one point their markets included providing flowers to Russia, Kuwait, Italy, Guam, Brazil, Chile, Puerto Rico, and Mexico among others. Farm Exports flower farms are primarily located in Ecuador; however, they market and sell Colombian, Californian, Costa Rican, New Zealand, Thai, and Israeli flowers. To further illustrate their growth, Farm Exports has expanded its line of wholesale flowers to include bulk wholesale flowers from Californian Boutique Growers. The new line includes spray kale, Chocolate Cosmos (a flower that smells like chocolate), and much more.

## FiftyFlowers.com Is Born

In 2002 Liza was approached by United Parcel Service (UPS) who presented her with a new program that consisted of shipping fresh flowers directly to the customer's doorstep in the U.S. Liza seized this opportunity to expand her company from Ecuador into the United States and thus merged the efforts of Farm Exports with an innovative Internet company. FiftyFlowers.com was born. This new Internet company ships flowers exclusively from farms she represents through Farm Exports to consumers' doorsteps throughout the United States, including Alaska, Hawaii, and Puerto Rico.

Much more planning was required for this second endeavor as it was unfamiliar territory for her. Liza had to study different transport methods among other things. Running an Internet company requires a completely different understanding of an industry. Meetings with experts to help her understand all aspects constituted her research. Planning lasted about five months, for a single product—a package of fifty roses. Since FiftyFlowers.com was one of the first Internet-based flower companies to ship directly, planning had to be done quickly so the company could keep that advantage. Once the basics were in place, the company started; a new niche was found.

FiftyFlowers.com did not get started without obstacles of its own. The main one was learning Web site development and management. When Liza made the decision to sell flowers via the Internet, the only online tool she fully understood was e-mail. Since Liza is an expert in exporting and importing flowers, this component of the business was not intimidating, but she found herself surrounded by technical issues about which she knew nothing. She had to become knowledgeable quickly. So she did everything in her power to make the site successful, but sometimes even her best efforts were not enough. During the first two weeks of operation, flowers were selling well. Everyone at the company was excited, but they soon discovered that they had failed to turn on the credit-card porthole;

consequently, the sales of the first two weeks were not deposited into their bank accounts. It was as though they had given the product away. Being an entrepreneur, you have to figure out operations as you go, an often intimidating and frustrating process, but trial and error mean that these mistakes become building blocks for learning how to make the business efficient and profitable.

## Exporting Flowers

Liza had to find a way to export the flowers while meeting both countries' standards. Now, the day-to-day routine is as follows: The boxes of flowers are scanned upon leaving the farm. They are scanned again before being loaded onto the airplane, and are scanned again once they arrive in the U.S. Then they are placed in a holding room where United States Department of Agriculture (USDA) inspectors check them randomly to make sure they do not contain drugs, diseases, or bugs. This, overwhelming as it may sound, is the process that has to be followed every day.

In December of 2003, Liza came back to the U.S. to visit her family and met the man who would become her husband, Blu Atwood. Then, in February of 2004, Liza moved back to the U.S. after laying solid foundations for both of her companies. She got married and moved to California with her husband and her daughter Alexandra.

## Networking and Marketing Go Hand in Hand

It was important to have a good foundation and grow slowly. Once the foundation was in place, the focus became generating buzz and forming valid partnerships. One such partnership was established while Liza was attending a luncheon with the Minister of Exterior Relations of Ecuador. She introduced Liza to a person connected to the Miss Universe pageant. Liza was eventually able to count this and other pageants as her clients.

Most of all, Liza wholeheartedly believed in and "could smell the success of FiftyFlowers.com." To create buzz at the beginning, Liza transformed herself into a walking billboard. Everywhere she went, whether it was a personal or business trip, she handed out marketing material, slipped simple advertisements into magazines, and spoke about her company to anyone who would listen. FiftyFlowers.com grew within a short period of time by becoming a company with a competitive edge in the industry.

## Support

Everyone with whom Liza has worked has affected her in some way, for better and for worse. She has embraced the positive and learned from the negative. Liza has looked to God over the years, and spiritual guidance has taught her to decipher the difference between the positive and the negative. With her company, she looks to and learns from the team she has in place. Each individual is an inspiration in her own way.

Liza's business support has come from attending conferences, reliance on team members, learning by mistakes, and most importantly, actively seeking knowledge on how to do something when faced with a problem. Liza's inner drive to keep the businesses moving forward has been the lifeline of her company.

The most influential people in Liza's life have been her parents and the woman her family adopted as grandmother. Her parents have encouraged Liza to work hard and be thankful for what she has, both while remaining honest. Ross and Sharon Roeser taught by example. Both finished their schooling while raising a family and are now successful doctors in education. As their children were growing up, Liza's parents insisted that they volunteer in the community. Liza and her two sisters volunteered at the local food shelters. Tasks such as these instilled in each of their children morals and compassion that remained with them throughout adulthood.

They reflect back on their parents' lead-by-example approach to teaching, and can truly state that they have lived the American Dream. Her parents remain together after many years of marriage, and now preach to their daughters the importance of not taking the easy way out of life.

Verna Treadwell is referred to as "Adopted Grandma" by Liza and her sisters. Verna met Liza's mother at a teacher's convention and became an immediate family friend. Verna filled the role of the family grandmother, which was a void for Liza since her blood grandmothers lived in different states. In turn, the Roesers provided Verna with the family that she never had. Verna never married; she is devoutly religious and a living example of honesty and kindness. She instilled strict morals in Liza and her sisters, and taught them the difference between right and wrong. She was a teacher, but her ability to teach went beyond the piano. Together, Verna and Mr. and Mrs. Roeser raised girls who made morally correct decisions.

## Overcoming Obstacles

Liza had to overcome cultural differences first when she moved to Ecuador and had to enter the Ecuadorian professional circle. When she moved to Ecuador, Liza only knew basic conversational Spanish, yet the language barrier was not the only problem. The cultural differences and gender differences proved to be bigger challenges. When she returned to the U.S., Liza faced similar challenges.

However, being bicultural helped her to better understand the flower industry. Being an expert in the field helped Liza make her way into the industry. In the U.S. flower industry, there are many flower professionals who rely heavily on Latin American suppliers. There are daily interactions with Latinos whose language most Anglos don't understand; they've generally never visited the countries or farms where the flowers are grown, and much less, understand the culture. After spending twelve years in the heart of the Ecuadorian and Colombian flower industry, not only is Liza well-informed, she is now a full-fledged Latina.

## Contributions

Liza considers her ability to give both Ecuadorian and American women the opportunity to be successful professionals while simultaneously being a good mother her biggest accomplishment. Now that she is a mother, she realizes even more how difficult it is to achieve this balance. Growing a nationwide clientele has proved to women everywhere that opportunities exist to achieve professional success while working at home.

Another contribution that goes hand in hand with having team members both in the States and internationally, is that she experiences the work environment in dual cultures. This is a difficult task to accomplish since each culture has its own *faux pas* as well as intricacies. However, this challenge is what adds energy to the daily activities.

Liza's company has chosen to direct monetary support and involve all employees in volunteering with several organizations, both to support Ecuador. The event Liza will be most proud of is the day they build a new home for *Milagros Preciosos*[13], the orphanage they support. That day will be one the most satisfying moments in her professional career. The company is striving to build the house by the end of 2007.

## Vision

The vision of the company has become clear within the last couple of years. The saying "two heads are better than one" truly applies to Liza's situation. Liza's husband who is a partner in the business has been an eye-opener for her as well as for the company. He is an expert in Internet marketing and offers many ideas and inspiration toward

---

[13] *Milagros Preciosos:* Precious Miracles

expansion—ideas that Liza says she would not have fully understood if it weren't for him. While sales have been growing three-hundredfold for the last three years, their way of operating has remained the same. They maintain a clear understanding of their goals and are laying the foundation to reach them. This includes formalizing their policies, developing a strategic plan, and creating an advisory board.

## Pride and Joy

Liza has felt a sense of personal pride numerous times over the years. The first compliment from a client because the company is able to help individuals create lasting memories while on a tight budget, *that* makes Liza smile.

The 10,000th sale milestone, marking 10,000 orders shipped, is "a heck of a lot of orders for a medium-sized business" according to Liza.

Watching beauty queens like Miss Universe, Miss USA, and Miss Teen USA walk across the stage carrying a bouquet made personally by Liza with FiftyFlower.com's roses was quite a milestone. It was an amazing feat to have her flowers broadcast internationally. Even though the company's name was not mentioned on television, the fact that they were present was sufficient to make for a proud moment.

Another memorable milestone was hiring the sixteenth woman of her team, which is illustrative of the company's ability to create work opportunities. Finally, the knowledge that her employees rely directly upon her and the success of the company to provide for their families, even though the responsibility now is shared with key leaders, it still is an intimidating feeling.

## Thinking Ahead

Liza's companies have been able to differentiate themselves from the competition due to excellent products and exceptional customer service. They take pride in the details. For example, buying online can be a very non-interactive way to purchase a product. You do not touch the product, do not see the physical store, or even speak with a company representative. When shopping for your wedding day, this can be nerve-racking. At FiftyFlowers.com, they recognize that people, especially brides, seek more personalized interaction, so they strive to achieve this personalization by contacting each client via telephone, offering expert wedding-flower advice via chat and phone conversations, and meeting them face-to-face at shows. They strive to participate in their lives as much as possible so the brides-to-be feel that they're not only purchasing the product, but getting to know the company as well.

The company's future centers wholly on growth. Their new Web site, which took twenty months of hard work to design, better targets their market and makes the experience more user-friendly. Another important aspect of the company is innovation. FiftyFlowers.com has been actively expanding their product line to include more sought-after fresh flowers, as well as do-it-yourself supplies and bridal favors. For the flower enthusiast, FiftyFlowers.com is adding a plethora of new products including a ready made wedding-flower package which gives a bride all she needs to create the wedding of her dreams.

## Harmony

According to Liza, her personal life is her professional life, and vice versa. The balance comes naturally and is achieved by having similar interests as her husband. Even though her husband works full time as a business-development marketer, he contributes at least twenty hours a week to FiftyFlowers.com. They share ideas and are equally committed to succeed. Together, they view this phase of their lives as the ideal time to grow in business. They currently have the energy and dedication required to tackle the challenge of expanding the company and pushing it to a new level of success. They both recognize that their hard work now will provide them with the life they imagine twenty years down the road.

Liza says, "God has blessed (and cursed) me with a never-ending inner drive for perfectionism." She is constantly striving for improvement, standing up for her morals, and reaching for success, no matter how many hurdles must be overcome. The mistakes she has made, and the difficult situations she has experienced have been converted into strength and character. Each day she feels enlightened with better direction for the company.

## Teaching in More Than One Way

Liza strongly believes in instructing her employees. She explains, "It is truly easy to talk to an employee and tell her what to do and how to do it, but although it may save time in the short run, it hinders the company instead of growing it." Explaining to employees how to do things, and more important, why it is necessary to do such things will give them a better understanding of the task, as well as how their role contributes to the overall efficiency of the company. One of the biggest challenges she encountered while teaching was understanding the bicultural differences between Latina and U.S. employees.

Liza also believes in contributing outside the company. Being socially responsible teaches social awareness and accountability to employees. In addition to contributing monetarily, Liza encourages Latina business owners to lead their teams by investing time and effort in helping social causes. By doing this herself, she has encouraged each of her team members toward self-realization and ultimately, happiness. The time spent together unifies her team. After spending a day at the orphanage, her employees are thankful and proud to be making a difference.

## Advice

As a woman, it is essential to believe in yourself. Liza says, "If you become intimidated by the challenges and overwhelming to-do lists, situations can become extremely frightening. Instead, make a long to-do list, prioritize the list, divide, and conquer. Try to take on the challenges one by one, rather than as a whole. Furthermore, focus on what is manageable while keeping an eye on the big picture so that your actions stay alert on the overall vision. This is not always easy. Find adamant determination within yourself. Couple this with a constant self-reminder that you are capable and that you WILL succeed, and not only will you reach your goals, you will exceed them."

## Conquering the World

There are many goals left unfinished, many ways to improve, and new projects to grow into. She will be a success "only once the world is conquered."

As any perseverant person knows, especially Liza, "Rome was not built in a day."

# Chapter 3:
# Martha de la Torre

Founder, Publisher, and CEO
*El Clasificado*
*www.elclasificado.com*

"I can still recall my confusion when I first learned in college what the term 'entrepreneur' meant. Why would someone *waste* a college degree by starting a business to face mostly risk and uncertainty?" It is hard to believe that these sentiments came from someone who would later found and lead the country's largest free, Spanish-language classifieds weekly. That someone is Martha de la Torre; the weekly publication is *El Clasificado*. But there were many twists and turns during Martha's transformation into a thriving entrepreneur.

## Endless Opportunities

Martha's parents were born and raised in Ecuador, where they lived during both the global economic depression and World War II. During this period in Ecuador, the opportunities for economic advancement were scarce, even for those with a good education. Believing that the United States offered endless opportunities, her parents moved to Los Angeles in the 1950s. They settled in East Los Angeles, got jobs, went to night school to learn English, and obtained other skills to make a decent living for the family. "A good education opens doors to opportunities," her parents believed.

Upon arriving in the US, they immediately invested in themselves and decided that their children could do anything they wanted as long as they studied hard and were good students. A year after her parents arrived in the US, Martha was born at White Memorial Hospital.

Martha's father had hopes of seeing his daughter grow up to become a doctor or a lawyer. Instead, Martha dreamed as a child of becoming a ballet dancer, a singer in musicals, or a Peace Corps volunteer who would travel the world. As she grew older, however, her strong imagination and interest in creative arts were tempered by her desire to ensure a good return on her parents' investment in her education. While Martha did not think of herself as a business person, it must have been inherent in her personality because she was already thinking about returns on investments, making budgets, cash flow forecasts and staying abreast of technology. One day before starting college, Martha created her first cash flow forecast to make sure that she could buy "key technology" items for her college days: a Texas Instruments calculator, a Smith Corona typewriter and her first 10-speed bicycle.

## Off to College

In 1977, Loyola Marymount University (LMU) had one of the strongest accounting programs in Los Angeles, and Martha felt that getting an accounting degree there would be a good move. Since she wanted to attend law school after college, Martha also felt that working in accounting would not only provide for a good living after college, but also a strong foundation for a future career in law.

Not knowing many accountants, Martha initially thought that accounting would be like learning bookkeeping: simple and straight-forward. Not surprisingly, learning the subject and getting A's in such a top-notch program proved much more challenging than she anticipated—particularly as she also worked her way through school.

## Arthur Young

The reputation of the LMU accounting program virtually guaranteed that most students past their junior year would have a good shot, if not a job, with a "Big 8" accounting firm. In the fall semester before her graduation, Martha interviewed on campus with various CPA firms and became interested in one firm in particular: Arthur Young (now known as Ernst and Young). She recalls meeting two Arthur Young female staff members and LMU alumni, Sue Alza and Kathy Neilsen, who took her out to lunch and later brought her to the Arthur Young office to meet Larry Behm, the managing partner of the Firm. Martha was impressed by Kathy and Sue's self assurance in communicating with Larry. At the time, it was uncommon to see female partners at other CPA firms, and staff could only address partners as "Mr."—if they had a chance to speak directly to partners at all. At Arthur Young, Kathy and Sue not only spoke to Larry with confidence, but they even addressed him by his first name. Martha liked what she saw and appreciated the firm's effort to make her feel comfortable and respected. She received a job offer that same day.

At Arthur Young, Martha started a corporate career that would eventually transform her from an *intrapreneur*—a person who can be innovative in a leadership position and grow a company but with the safety net of a weekly paycheck—into an entrepreneur. Working at Arthur Young for the first few years felt like going to graduate business school, but with the benefit of getting paid to learn while gaining exposure to different types of business. Martha soon realized that attending law school was no longer necessary or desirable; she was promoted to manager in five years, and foresaw a bright future ahead of her in accounting.

Martha was an Arthur Young manager for two years, during which she built upon her formative LMU education and began to transform into a more complete businesswoman. Since she would often attend board meetings and conduct presentations in front of CEOs at Arthur Young, Martha gained confidence as an effective client advisor, problem-solver and team leader. The Arthur Young philosophy and principles would prove extremely valuable later in her corporate career and as an "accidental" entrepreneur: think out of the box, manage your business better than your competitors do, train and nurture employees into superb performers and, above all, be good to your employees. While at Arthur Young, Martha noticed and was fascinated by the growing media interest in the Hispanic market. Hispanics were increasingly featured in many mainstream publications as Latino art and culture were integrated into the general media. The anticipated growth in the Hispanic market, coupled with her bicultural background and skills, prompted Martha to collect data and information about Hispanics, and motivated her to explore business opportunities to tap the nascent but emerging market.

Things at Arthur Young were going very well for Martha. She reached two of her life's high points during this time: She had become a manager at only twenty-five years old, and she had met her future husband. Martha enjoyed the team spirit, intellectual stimulation, intensity, and fast pace at Arthur Young, which also included working 24/7 before the concept became popular.

Despite her success at Arthur Young, Martha anticipated that continuing in her current career would make it difficult to one day start and raise a family as the demands of a top-notch accounting firm would only increase with greater seniority. While Arthur Young was already offering flexible schedules to women in management positions, Martha (still in her twenties) did not look forward to balancing the rigors of work with the demands of raising a family. After seven and a half years at Arthur Young, Martha decided that it was a good time to move on and leave the CPA firm world for brighter pastures.

## A New Opportunity

At Arthur Young, Martha had taken on *La Opinión*, the largest Spanish daily, as one of her clients. Martha believed that *La Opinión* had a lot of potential for growth, so when they asked her to be their Chief Financial Officer at the time of her departure from Arthur Young, she seized the opportunity. She was only twenty eight. Martha knew she could help *La Opinión* grow in the booming Latino climate.

The new challenge at *La Opinión* further exposed Martha to the inner workings of an organization that catered to the Hispanic market and the challenges of building cost-effective operational infrastructures. It also gave Martha an opportunity to hone her skills in cash flow and payroll management and overall financial administration.

Upon joining *La Opinión,* Martha knew that she needed to develop a thorough understanding of newspaper operations. She achieved this by interviewing and gathering insights from members in every department. Coupled with significant research and analysis, Martha developed a business plan to secure a multimillion-dollar loan for a new press. She was determined to make an impact with her new employer.

She would soon find another high-impact area upon which to focus. Growing circulation is the key to success for any newspaper. Curiously, as an advisor to *La Opinión* prior to becoming the CFO, Martha had not been fully aware of the limitations in the company's distribution system. In conversations with the circulation manager, Martha quickly learned that the sixty-year-old daily with close to 70,000 newspapers in circulation only had two street racks! One rack was located at the newspaper building's entrance; the second, in front of City Hall. Under Martha's guidance, *La Opinión* bought a few hundred street racks and placed them in strategic locations, which made the paper available to a greater number of readers throughout Southern California.

Growing *La Opinión* was an ongoing challenge. The publication had many decades of history and tradition which, in many ways, were also obstacles to effecting positive change. After two years at *La Opinión,* Martha grew weary of the internal change resistance that she faced and decided to leave in 1987. Shortly after leaving *La Opinión*, Martha briefly considered attending graduate business school to become an investment banker, with the idea of working on mergers and acquisitions that targeted the Latino market. However, another idea ended up capturing her passion and imagination: Martha began writing the business plan for a free, Spanish-language, home-delivered publication.

## From Business Plan to Business

In 1988, while writing this plan, Martha felt like she was developing a project for any one of her clients, for someone else to take the risk. But what *did* immediately resonate with her was the tremendous business opportunity that the Latino community presented. Many products successfully marketed in English were not marketed in Spanish. Martha thought about her parents emigrating from Ecuador and facing challenges in integrating into a new society. What kind of informational resource could make the lives of Latino immigrants easier? This question was the catalyst for what would later become the "PennySaver" in Spanish, *El Clasificado®*, which also included tips on parenting, health, and education.

*El Clasificado* evolved from the idea that there was a lack of free Latino-community publications outside of downtown Los Angeles. The English-language PennySaver seemed to thrive and it made sense that a Spanish version that included community editorials to help recent immigrants learn how to improve their lives would also succeed. Martha chose the PennySaver format because it would be easy to replicate using newly available desktop-publishing systems. She says, "It's ironic that I am the publisher of Spanish-language publications considering that Spanish is not my dominant language. But from this obstacle came an opportunity: Because of my moderate Spanish-language skills I chose to start a Spanish-language 'shopper' magazine instead of a more complex and artsy publication, as I'd first envisioned. How hard could it be to proofread classifieds?"

Martha left the writing and editing of the short consumer editorials to her father. He was recently retired and was willing to help in any way he could. Martha's father enjoyed providing advice on parenting, health, and even on transitioning to the American lifestyle.

Martha set several parameters for her publication: It had to be free, community-oriented, in Spanish, and contain short easy-to-read editorials. In addition, the publication was zoned to give advertisers greater geographic coverage and flexibility. Months were spent working on refining the business plan and financial projections. Laptop computers had just arrived on the market but there was no Internet yet available for research, prompting Martha to spend hours in libraries gathering demographic information available on microfiche.

After months of planning and preparation, Martha was able to secure investors to fund the venture. The former CPA and CFO who as a college student was once confused about the term "entrepreneur" was now about to become one. There was no turning back; Martha had grown too passionate about *El Clasificado*, which would provide access to services, products and information for people like her parents. Martha launched *El Clasificado* on May 4, 1988.

*El Clasificado's* operations commenced with high expectations but limited start-up capital and growing funding complications. The company was only able to raise about $350,000 in start-up capital, a far cry from the $600,000 to $1,000,000 anticipated in her business plan. After her initial investors pulled out, she began to raise money from family and friends on a weekly basis, in order to make up the significant shortfall in sales revenue. Cash flow projections were made by her daily. She became the salesperson and marketer while her husband, Joseph Badame, took care of operations after his day job. They found customers by prospecting and selling door to door as well as through telemarketing, and found leads through the media. Because the 1980s were a time of rapid growth, Martha developed an aggressive business plan to which she closely adhered. However, her company struggled initially. The recession of the early

90s compounded the company's difficulties, prolonging the number of years before they were profitable.

## Stand and Deliver

It was around that time that Martha was inspired by the film *Stand and Deliver.* The movie showed how one person can affect the lives of others by challenging them to work hard and to believe in themselves. Martha also understood that there were bright and talented students, not only in East Los Angeles, but in inner cities nationwide, who just needed an opportunity to flourish. She chose to recruit local high school students because she knew they were intelligent, energetic, and talented.

Recruiting Garfield High School students turned out to be mutually beneficial: The students contributed energy and computer skills, while Martha provided them the opportunity to earn a weekly paycheck, develop professional skills, and earn advancement within the company. Martha proudly states that a handful of these students are still with *El Clasificado* today and hold management-level positions in the company. They are making enormous contributions to help position themselves as the leading Hispanic multimedia-solutions organization in the country.

## What's in a Name?

*El Clasificado* has often been criticized for not having movie stars on its covers, not being glossy, being too simple, and having a mouthful for a name. Now, the company name is a valuable and sought-after asset. Last year alone, the company spent over $100,000 in legal fees to defend the *El Clasificado* trademark in the U.S. and abroad. Today Martha chuckles when people comment on her vision and the perfect name for the publication. *El Clasificado* may not be fancy or glossy, but it has delivered just what the market needs and wants.

## Continuous Changes

According to Martha, to work at *El Clasificado,* one has to be on top of the continuous changes in the industry while simultaneously keeping alive the traditions to which the readers are accustomed. Finally, to work for *El Clasificado,* one also has to be ready to multi-task. Without enough staff for an ever-growing number of events, projects, and promotions, one has to be ready for anything. Those who work at *El Clasificado* are able to handle the workload because they have a passion for what they do. They know that no matter what the difficulty, the value of the outcome always exceeds the obstacles they had to overcome. The company continues to grow each year, providing employees with an opportunity to grow.

However, growth was not always consistent. When English-language newspapers felt the recession in 1990, classified advertising (a traditional indicator of future economic activity) fell markedly in newspapers like the *Los Angeles Times.* That recession had hit the Hispanic market earlier and harder. *El Clasificado* was launched in 1988 and, shortly after the first issues were distributed, the recession took hold of Southern California. The challenges to Martha's business undertaking were immense. She was forced to sell her home and car and move in with her parents to keep the business going. Martha even took a part-time job as a CPA to make ends meet. There were times she didn't think she'd see the light at the end of the tunnel. Customers who placed ads when the publication was first launched would say, "The publication looks good, but we're not getting any results on our ads." But the dream never died. The recession caused them to take a hard look at the business model and chart a new course.

## The Turning Point

All throughout the struggles that the company faced, Martha remained in love with her product and company. Her love deepened as she increasingly witnessed the results delivered to customers, the positive and team-oriented work environment, and the things the company was doing to help the community. All these achievements represented a major success milestone for the company.

But financial success would only come later and as result of a desperate survival move to reduce expenses. Instead of delivering *El Clasificado* to individual homes (as they had done since starting the company), they arranged to have it dropped off at various locations such as local meat markets, bakeries, and independent shops. Delivery costs plummeted from $35 per 1,000 copies to $10 per 1,000—essentially cutting costs by more than half. This new distribution model began to give their clients better results. However, it wasn't until 1993 that they started a database for their distribution drops. From this database, they began to develop a system for monitoring drops and returns. Then in 1995, they started investing in street racks and third-party distributors who would place their magazines in major outlets like Kmart and Sav-On Drugs.

## Positive Growth

The positive trajectory that resulted from this developed distribution model has not stopped. *El Clasificado* has experienced over 20% growth year after year since 2000. Martha is very grateful to her husband Joe, also a CPA, who manages and builds on this model every year, ensuring that their clients get maximum exposure for their advertising. Now *El Clasificado* has over 8,500 circulation locations throughout the community, most of which are street racks. In many places like Los Angeles, Orange County, and the Inland Empire, *El Clasificado* was the first Spanish-language publication to install street racks. Those installations have been a major investment requiring constant maintenance but are key to their successful growth over the past ten years.

*El Clasificado's* award-winning circulation system and strategy, the key to the company's continued success, was developed and is currently managed by Joe, who is also the company's COO and cofounder. In the early years, Martha's family managed circulation. Now, Joe is fully responsible for this operation and spends a significant amount of time developing relationships with the business owners who let them place their magazine racks inside their stores. Other publications, including *La Opinión*, have asked *El Clasificado* for distribution services, but this is not the company's focus. "We have enough opportunities with our own multiple publications and have plans to expand outside of Los Angeles," our accidental entrepreneur states.

## Exciting Times

These are exciting times at *El Clasificado*, and the future is bright. The company recently moved to a new building where they are also hosting invitation-only mini concerts for *Al Borde*, their Latin alternative publication with roots in the alternative Spanish-rock movement, which *El Clasificado* acquired in 2001. Due to its steady growth over the past few years, the company faces new opportunities virtually every week and is continuously implementing innovative processes to handle new products and services. Martha keeps a daily focus on sales, marketing, and community relations among other CEO duties.

Currently, *El Clasificado* is on the verge of a major strategic push outside of Los Angeles. Fortunately, their team of C-level executives, along with the next level of directors and managers, possess the talent Martha believes will lead *El Clasificado* to become the global leader of Spanish-language grassroots media solutions in print, Internet, events, and mobile. In the year 2000, the company had $2,000,000 in sales, $9,000,000 in 2006, and they expect to reach across California to double revenues by 2009. The future looks bright for *El Clasificado*, not only because its people have worked so hard to make it a successful business, but because they help their community as well. A good example of this is the *Su Socio de Negocios* seminar series presented by *El Clasificado*. *Su Socio de Negocios* is a series of free grassroots community events that provide guidance in Spanish on how to start and operate a business.

Thanks to the event's success, Martha decided to repeat the grassroots events formula which provides immediate access to specific services in an interactive, non-intimidating platform, while focusing each time on a different segment of our community. This resulted in *Quinceañera* and *Hogar, Mi Dulce Hogar,* two additional expos designed to offer assistance to families who are about to celebrate their daughter's quinceañera, and first-time home buyers, respectively.

## Contributions

Martha says she is very proud of *El Clasificado's* economic contributions to a country that provides opportunities to so many. Now in its nineteenth year, *El Clasificado* currently employs more than one hundred talented professionals. In addition to her company's economic contributions, Martha is also proud of the community outreach that her company provides such as mentorship, promoting higher learning, and informing the public through consumer-awareness editorials. Martha gets tremendous satisfaction from being able to give something back to the country that embraced her parents and afforded them so much.

In the spirit of reciprocity, Martha spends about 20 percent of her time each week on community activities with nonprofit boards of directors, on which she sits. Other community organizations that have solicited her assistance include the L.A. County Education Foundation, Don Bosco Technical Institute, L.A. Family Housing, the L.A. Child Guidance Clinic, and Loyola Marymount University's Mexican American Alumni Association (MAAA). Martha was recently appointed to LMU's Board of Regents, thanks to her resolute commitment to her alma mater. Martha also speaks at community events that inspire Latinos to seek higher education and improve their lives. Such work within the community does not simply fill Martha with personal satisfaction, but it is also creates many opportunities to meet and partner with other businesses.

## Mentors

Fortunately, Martha has had many mentors throughout her life, beginning with those at her alma mater, LMU. According to Martha, Fr. Merrifield, former chancellor and president of LMU, saw *El Clasificado*'s potential for success and inspired her to keep going despite her initial apprehension about the venture. Dr. Fred Kiesner, chair for the Center of Entrepreneurship and professor of Business Management at LMU, and Mr. George Dasaro, LMU professor of accounting, have helped honor and recognize *El Clasificado*, not only for its financial success, but also for its success in aligning their business objectives with community service.

At Arthur Young, Martha had seven and a half empowering years under the guidance and training of many experienced mentors who opened her eyes to the business community of Los Angeles—one to which she never imagined belonging. Martha says, "I am very grateful for my years at Arthur Young, particularly to my old friend and mentor Barry Franzen." At Arthur Young, Martha was transformed into a businesswoman with leadership skills and experience in a variety of industries with economic challenges. Consequently, she was ready to take her leadership role in business when the right opportunities appeared.

Martha was also introduced to a host of professional mentors through the Association of Free Community Papers (AFCP), which *El Clasificado* joined in 2001. The training and networking opportunities that resulted from the AFCP conventions helped Martha achieve enormous growth and also resulted in mentoring relationships with experienced industry insiders like Dick Mandt, Pete Gorman, Orestes Baez, Carlos Guzman from Harte Hanks, and Peter Lamb, the company's longtime strategic consultant.

Martha's husband is also her mentor. She admits, "Joe is my strength when I feel that the external pressures are becoming too heavy. He always helps lift the load and we always seem to proceed ahead even stronger." Martha and Joe have been happily married for sixteen years. Also indispensable are her parents and brothers. They have all helped financially, proffered advice, and offered expertise.

## Accolades

One of the accomplishments of which Martha is very proud is the continued guidance she has provided to the high school students and young college graduates who she has personally mentored. Through great coaching and patience, Martha has successfully guided many inner-city students to graduate and pursue management careers at *El Clasificado*. According to Martha, she looks for potential skills in every employee and provides training to facilitate everyone's growth to their maximum potential. "By mentoring young women, sharing our stories, and continuing to create job opportunities through our businesses, we can help Latina women learn to empower themselves," says Martha. She gets excited whenever she meets young women who, despite struggles and limited finances, have finished college and are passionate about their futures. Martha tries to either create a job opportunity at her company or facilitate introductions for them at other companies where they can flourish.

Although Martha has received various awards and accolades during almost two decades with *El Clasificado*, the award of which she is the most proud is the Inner City 100 Award because it underscores the role that *El Clasificado* plays in the community. In 2004, *El Clasificado* was honored as one of the fastest-growing inner-city businesses in the United States at the Inner-City 100 Awards Summit in Boston. The Inner City 100 recognizes businesses that make a positive contribution to the country's economy by creating jobs and empowering the inner-city communities.

In May 2007, *El Clasificado* was chosen as a finalist for the Ernst & Young Entrepreneur of the Year (EOY) Award. This award, in existence for more than two decades, recognizes excellence in business leadership. Previous winners of this prestigious award include Michael Dell, founder of Dell Computers; Pierre Omidyar, co-founder of eBay; and Jim McCann of 1-800-Flowers.com.

## Business Ethics

Besides Martha's experience, training, and the continued support from her family, she attributes her success to her business ethics. According to Martha, she does not take anything for granted—not her customers, employees, suppliers, or business supporters. It is important that everyone is treated fairly and with due respect. Every transaction has to be a win-win situation.

## Strategic Alliances

After having been through so much with her company, Martha does not want to have to sell it to grow. She plans to create strategic alliances that will help them reach their vision. *El Clasificado* wants to be the leader in connecting buyers and sellers in the U.S. Latino market through classifieds in print, online and mobile technology while contributing to the communities that they service.

*El Clasificado* is always trying to help their readers learn to find better careers, improve their education, start their own businesses or help their children be more successful in school. Martha and her company want to help the Latino community learn to help themselves. Very often *El Clasificado* directs editorials to mothers, grandmothers, aunts, and sisters because, in our culture, women are often the spearheads of change for success. Martha always enjoys taking the opportunity to tell the story of *El Clasificado* from the challenges they faced as a nascent entity within the Latino community to the success they are currently experiencing. Such opportunities remind her not to take success for granted; she remains inspired to share her knowledge and insights with other would-be entrepreneurs.

## Being Number One

*El Clasificado* is currently the country's largest free, Spanish-language classifieds weekly. Not only does Martha want to continue to hold this spot, but her company plans to expand its geographic and Internet-based reach across California and throughout the West Coast, eventually spanning the country and the entire globe. In addition to expanding , *El Clasificado* is increasingly positioned as the leading multimedia platform that offers advertising opportunities through print and online display and classified ads, sponsored events, special print sections, street-team promotions, Websites and mobile services.

The breadth and depth of these plans could be daunting for most entrepreneurs. However, Martha is confident that her management team has put together the staff and organization that enable their vision of creating bridges that inspire and empower the Hispanic community.

On the personal side, Martha wants to achieve a better work-lifestyle balance. She and her husband love their company and what they do. They generally need to pry themselves away from the business to enjoy more opportunities to spend time nurturing the quieter, more personal aspects of their lives such as spending time with their families. Her nieces and nephews are entering their teens, and Martha wants to make sure that she is always available to help them become happy and successful adults, as well as share in their life experiences when possible. Every day of life is a gift and they want to live it properly and completely.

Martha's successful journey as an entrepreneur has taken a lot of honest self-analysis. Throughout this journey, she has had to consistently assess and refresh her skills, her strengths, her weaknesses, and most of all, the level of risk that she is willing to take. The difficult years that she faced in the '90s put a lot of pressure, both financial and emotional, on her family and friends. It took a lot of self-sacrifice, humility, and tenacity to persevere. Martha and her strong support system that includes family, friends, and employees have all made *El Clasificado* an incredibly successful publication—and a truly inspirational story for those who may be "confused" if not daunted by the term "entrepreneur."

# Chapter 4:
# Patricia Pliego-Stout

President
The Alamo Travel Group
*www.alamotravel.com*

Patricia Pliego-Stout is an extraordinary woman. She comes from entrepreneurial blood. This thriving entrepreneur has lived a life of seized opportunities, and has survived in the male-dominated world of travel because she is strong woman, not in spite of it.

## Journey to the Unknown

First on her list of life-changing highlights, was moving to the United States. Although a difficult process for most immigrants, it was an uncomplicated process for Pat. She and her husband moved to San Antonio, Texas, with the intention of opening construction companies. But this was not her first visit to the country. When she was younger, she did a lot of her shopping in San Antonio. The fact that she knew the city well and that it had daily flights to Mexico City made it the ideal place to settle for her future business ventures. The need to be close to an airport with flights that could take her back to Mexico City was important because of Pat's commitment to her family. She wanted the ability to visit her parents in a matter of hours.

The need to remain connected to her family has its roots in Pat's parents. Her mother, a lifelong housewife, raised Pat and her sister while her father ran his own business. Pat has entrepreneurial blood running deep inside her. Her father owned a furniture manufacturing company. They made everything from sofas to lamps. This was Pat's first exposure to the world of business.

When she was a young girl, Pat worked at the manufacturing company and was paid for her work. She liked helping for that reason and also because she was allowed to do things outside of the house. Growing up in Mexico, she felt that being the head of a family and being responsible for a business was too much for a woman. She grew up thinking it was a man's job, not daring to think that one day she would be involved in a similar pursuit. Women of Pat's generation were born and raised to get married, have children, and live happily ever after. For this reason, in her youth, Pat never fancied herself as anything other than a happy housewife with lots of children.

## Short-Lived Education

However, Pat was given a great opportunity when she enrolled at the Universidad Autónoma de Mexico in 1968. That year saw the riots at Tlatelolco, a confrontation between students and police that resulted in the deaths of hundreds of people by the government for political reasons. Pat's father feared for her safety so she was not allowed to return to school and did not receive a degree. Constantly learning new things was so important to her that she decided to learn foreign languages to complement her education. She learned Italian, French, and English.

Pat studied business administration and accounting, excelling in both. Accounting was especially enjoyable, which is why she became supervisor of the companies for which she worked, including MASECA, Mexico Office, Xerox de Mexico, and Colgate. Even though she didn't think she wanted to be in charge when she was a little girl, as a young adult, she liked telling people what to do. Working on projects that related to finance gave Pat a lot of pleasure.

She even met the man who would become her husband at one of the companies she worked.

## Moving to the U.S.

Pat was married in March of 1973 and moved to the United States one year and one month later. Upon her arrival, Pat immediately found a job when she learned a nearby petroleum corporation was looking for a bilingual secretary. At the time in San Antonio, there were not many people who spoke fluent Spanish, let alone had the ability to write, read, or translate it; Pat got the job in 1974.

She worked for a couple of petroleum companies even after she had her two children, while her husband ran a construction business owned by his father. Once the construction companies were doing well, they decided to invest in the travel business. The couple bought a travel-agency franchise and opened two small travel agencies. Pat's marriage was dissolving when, in 1981, she was presented with the opportunity to buy one of the agencies; she realized she could become independent by becoming a business owner. Having a gift for administration and financing really helped her during the early stages of the business, but not everything was that easy. With little computer savvy, she had to teach herself how to operate a computer for business purposes. She also had to teach herself how to market the business, and even how to prepare taxes. Fortunately, she had good friends, as well as a CPA who helped her along her journey.

## Selling the Business

Amazingly enough, eighteen months later, she received an offer from one of her clients who wanted to buy the business. Pat was in the process of divorcing her husband and found an opportunity to go back to Mexico, so she accepted the offer to sell her travel business for cash. Pat sold the agency, received her divorce settlement, and purchased a CD; at this point she had accumulated a substantial amount of money. Pat decided to visit her relatives in Mexico. Although she was comforted by her relatives, it came as a surprise that they had mapped out her life. While having breakfast with her family, they told her, "We're going to find a house for you. You'll have a maid. There is a great school for the children down the street, and we've also found a driver for you." But Pat was not having any of it; that was not what she was looking for. Pat remembers many decisions that were not made by her, but by her family. At the age of thirty-nine, she had never lived alone, never really done anything on her own, so she decided that it was the right time to do something for herself and her children. At the same time, she wanted her children to maintain a relationship with their father.

When she returned to San Antonio, Pat's ex-husband asked for help with another travel agency he owned because he was having trouble working on both the agencies and his construction business. Pat was promised half of the agency if she turned it into a profitable business. After two and one-half years of hard work that led to great profits, the time came for Pat and her husband to part ways again. When she asked for her half of the agency, she was met with one of the most upsetting and disappointing answers of her life. He had decided that he hadn't really meant it when he promised her half of the company. It was one of the most heartbreaking experiences any-one could ever encounter, but it did not break Pat's spirit. Her strong will and entrepreneurial determination pushed her to go on with her life.

## Dramatic Changes

In spite of the seemingly insurmountable setback, Pat decided to branch out on her own. It took three years of very difficult negotia-tions but in 1990, she bought the corporation, acquired the name of "Alamo Travel" and became sole owner. The decision to acquire her own business was one of the most difficult but also most rewarding of her life. It was an exhilarating feeling to know that she was finally in charge of her own destiny. With no more husband or boss, she had to answer to no one but herself. It was a very exciting time in her life.

Pat continued to work very hard on her own for many years. At one point she thought, "There has to be a better way of doing this." That is when she got involved with the San Antonio Hispanic Chamber of Commerce and the City of San Antonio, as well as attending many seminars and presentations ranging in topic from what to call your business to how to develop it. One day while attending a seminar hosted by the Chamber and the City on how to become a government contractor, Pat had a revelation. After the seminar ended, she knew she had found her true niche.

Since that day, her life has changed dramatically. Soon after the seminar, she attended a training session with the Department of Economic Development in the City of San Antonio. Thankfully, Pat had friends who were already in government contracting and they became her mentors. One of those mentors was Rosalinda Manzano, who said to Pat, "If you're serious, if you're going to do this, it's going to be tough, but I'm willing to help you because it's very hard to find somebody who wants to do this work. I know that a lot of people want to get started in this kind of business but since it's so difficult, they just give up because they have to certify their company with several different agencies."

Pat knew nothing about government contracting. She didn't even know she could have her business certified as a woman-owned business, and that is where she started. After certifying herself as minority business owner with San Antonio, and then with the SBA as an 8(a) contractor, her mentors and friends helped her look for contracts. In 1993 they found one that came from Fort Worth, Texas, for the General Services Administration (GSA). In those days, it consisted of five hundred pages that had to be typed. There was no filling anything out on a computer; it was horrendous. So she said to Rosalinda, "I think you were right; this is not for me."

To which Rosalina replied, "No. We're not expecting you to know how to fill these out. We will get somebody to help you, but you're going to have to spend some money."

The news was terrifying to Pat since she was told that she would get a consultant who charged $25 an hour. Then, to make matters worse, she was told the woman was going to be in her office anywhere between a week and a month. She did the math and almost fainted; eight hours is a lot of money—$200 a day! Her mentor told her, "You will never regret it" and it's true; Pat never regretted spending that money. The woman stayed in her office, learned about the travel business, prepared the bids, and miraculously, Alamo Travel was awarded the contract.

## Lucky First-Timer

As a first-time bidder, Pat was able to secure a contract valued at close to $4 million. She considers herself a lucky first-timer, but also acknowledges that she had a lot of help. Everyone from the Hispanic Chamber, her lawyer, her CPA, the people from the City, all wanted her to be successful. Pat was beyond thrilled; she told people about the bid and how amazing it was. Unfortunately, the enthusiasm was short-lived. Her agency was neither properly prepared nor trained for such a contract.

There were people out there who did not want Pat to succeed. The contracting officer with the General Services Administration was one of them. He didn't train Pat's agency. She believes part of the reason was because she was a minority, she was new, and they wanted the incumbent to get the contract. The contracting officer gave Pat and her employees a two-hour briefing. It is impossible for anyone to learn how to administer a contract or provide services to a contracting clerk in that short amount of time. Usually, a business is given thirty to forty-five days to transition with training. Being the resourceful woman that she is, Pat asked her employees to work through the weekend to prepare for the coming week. She also hired people to work after hours to create profiles for each customer of each agency. The contracting officer told Pat that on Monday, twelve hundred customers were going to call. Just before she left, she said, "Guess what? I don't think you can handle it."

## Loyal Clientele

On a different occasion, Pat vividly remembers being in an auditorium where the contracting officer introduced her to the agencies. The officer said to everyone, "Well, this is the company that got the award but I don't think they're going to be your permanent service provider." Pat was astonished. How could a government contracting officer be so unprofessional? This type of unconscionable behavior would have chased many out of business, but Pat operates differently. She would have had every right to give up after trying to negotiate such seemingly insurmountable challenges. Years later some of the customers who were there—and who to this day continue to be her customers—told her they were shocked that the officer had been so unprofessional. They had felt bad for her and decided to be patient and help her. Loyal customers are part of what keep Pat, and other entrepreneurs like her, going every day.

However, that was not the only type of abuse—she calls it entrepreneurial abuse-so she called the people who were helping her. They told her she didn't have to take their mistreatment because they weren't even paying her; the GSA owed her a lot of money. But her contracting officer had the nerve to say, "That's what happens to people like you. You should not be involved in government contracting if you don't even know how to send your bills to be paid." Pat admits that she broke down and cried at that point. Even the strongest spirits can be bent sometimes. Compounded with the officer, the incumbent protested her award twice.

The protest was devastating to Pat; she was accused of not being the sole owner of the company among other false accusations. However, just as before, people who believed in her and wanted her to succeed came to Pat's aid. Her lawyer helped her, as did friends who knew about contacts, and Pat was able to follow through on her contract. So it was not a pleasant experience, but even through adversity, this strong entrepreneur was able to make her mark. It was the first time in the GSA's history that a minority, Latina small-business owner had received such an award. The year was 1994.

## The Government

After surviving that contract, Pat was ready for anything, eventually moving on to contracts with the Department of the Defense, and even NASA. This part of Pat's journey started when she joined the Society of Government Travel Professionals (SGTP). She started going to the meetings to learn, asking questions and generally immersing herself. After a couple of years, around 1998, a man asked Pat if he could visit her office. Having a stranger ask you that question can be somewhat disconcerting and Pat asked him what he wanted. He responded, "Would you entertain the idea of becoming a Defense contractor?" To which Pat replied, "Not me, I'm very happy with my contracts." Then he countered, "Those contracts don't last forever; you should seize this opportunity. You're a small business and you have an excellent reputation, so you would be great for this."

Thanks to her instincts, she agreed to meet with him. He went to San Antonio, checked her office very thoroughly, and examined her employees, operation, reports, and even computers. He then told her he was a consultant who worked for small-business owners and that he now wanted to work for Pat. He would help her identify proposals, understand the contracting language, and determine if she qualified for the contracts. The most difficult part of a government contract is the reporting process. She told him that she was still having difficulty with the GSA; she didn't want to get involved with something even more complicated. His response was that he would train and teach her staff to take care of that particular aspect of contracting.

## Building Relationships

Once again, as a first-time bidder, Pat was able to procure a $6 million contract. And it was no ordinary client; it was the United States Air Force. That was her first contract and she had very little time to get started: three weeks. This type of contracting was also unknown to Pat, but this time there was something different. The man who offered to help her was actually training her. Another thing that helped Pat through these trying times was something she learned early on in her childhood. Pat always paid attention to instructions; whatever her parents and teachers told her to do, she did. She believes that the ability to listen and follow instructions, to do what you're expected to do, whatever it may be, has helped her a lot in life. Through this ability, she is able to listen and perform, which is exactly what she did with the government. That is an excellent parallel.

It's a cultural thing. But Pat had never said that to anyone before. She shared this bit of insight because when people ask her, "isn't it difficult?" Pat's internal answer is "Oh, my god, it's extremely difficult." But what she actually answers is that you have to build a relationship with the government, without questioning. That ability comes from her upbringing and it has been tremendously helpful in dealing with the government. Unfortunately, one can also appreciate that times have changed. We're losing a lot of those values. Pat can see that in her daughters; with them she says, "You have to ask them to do something at least three times; with me, only one time."

Things were going well for Pat. Her contract with the Air Force was finalized in October of 2000, and she had obtained additional contracts. But her sense of security was shattered on September 11, 2001. Pat had mixed feelings of pride, fear, and sadness, and realized she had a role to play.

## Contracts Awarded

After September 11, Pat thought she was going to lose her business because of the damage that had been done to the travel industry in general. However, when things started moving along, her consultant said, "Let's bid for as many contracts as we see coming down the pipeline." So they did. The result was that the company was awarded all of the contracts upon which they bid. At that time, she thought she was "going to die" because she still had the GSA contract, as well as her regular travel agency. On top of all of that, she had to open seven travel agencies in seven different Air Force bases the same day. Her managers and her consultant made it possible. Lackland Air Force Base nominated Alamo Travel for the Military Surface Deployment and Distribution Command (SDDC) Quality Award for outstanding service to the Department of Defense during 2003. They received the award because they were prompt, did not make mistakes, saved the government money, and responded to emergencies and problems within 24 hours. Today, Pat runs sixteen Air Force travel-service offices.

The process is no less complicated once the contract has been obtained. According to Pat, once you get the award, you travel to an Air Force base and set up business by opening up a travel-service office. Pat brings along her own employees while also trying to hire from among those on base. She also brings along new equipment such as computer hardware and software necessary to the running of the office. It is a separate business from the government, but they use the government's premises. Pat's travel agency issues tickets for official travel to anybody who works on the base. By contract, they only use her agency. Alamo Travel is available twenty-four hours per day, seven days per week. Opening an office on government premises the first time was difficult. Even gaining admittance to the Air Force base was a new experience. Everyone needs to have an ID. The pressure is tremendous since Pat and her employees share the same office with government employees. The bases have a certain level of security clearance and my employees are only allowed to go in and out of their premises directly. The rigidity of the rules and regulations means that Pat's agency has to be very careful in everything they do. Pat follows every instruction that is given to her and makes her employees do the same.

The government pays service fees for each ticket issued. This is known as a negotiated government contract based on service fees. One thing Pat strongly believes is that small-business owners have an advantage on pricing because they don't hire extra personnel or have several layers of management or vice presidents. They usually have only the necessary number of hard-working people. Pat is proud of not having "prima donnas all over the place," and thanks to that, she doesn't have to make frivolous payments of money.

## No Extra Layers

There are no extra layers in her employee ranks either, even though Pat owns nineteen offices. She has managers in each of the offices who report to the General Manager and the Operations Manager. Pat knows everyone she hires. Supervision is no longer part of Pat's job description. The technology has become so complicated that she's not "involved in that as much anymore." She's busy working with other parts of the company such as interacting with the government, working on bids, visiting people at the Air Force bases, and taking care of problems personally. That's one thing she's realized people like: Pat's company takes care of problems within twenty-four hours and if necessary, Pat or one of her managers travels to take care of the situation. That rapid response has put them on the map as excellent service providers, but the feminine touch Pat brings to her company has helped her as well.

In the travel business, one has to be patient, and learn how to listen. Thankfully, those are qualities that most women possess—especially when they are mothers. Her ex-husband once told her that this business was not for him, declaring, "I have no patience. I cannot be doing this. This is absolutely too difficult." There are a lot of men in the travel business, but if you ask Pat, she'll tell you that the most successful small-business contractors are women. They have the patience that is needed to take care of this very difficult business. She says that when you have a need and you have to fulfill that need, the obstacles become challenges and then you get used to obstacles in everything you do because it's part of doing business. Pat says that she's realized that her job, although emotionally taxing, physically tiring, and often generally monotonous and difficult, is easier to understand and negotiate as a woman.

## Female Agents

Alamo Travel's best travel agents are women, and Pat believes it is because of their caring nature. She believes that if she were a man (while this is not true of all men), she probably would have been more aggressive. She would have been more ambitious for power. But Pat was never out to become a millionaire. According to her, "Men always like to go to the next level, to make more money, or to be recognized. And another difference between men and women is that women are usually interested in the learning process. We like to grow more in that respect." Latinas are the fastest-growing sector of the economy, and Pat thinks it's because we work very hard. Many of us have to sustain our families, and the training process is how one is able to grow a business. Pat didn't know anything about travel; all she knew was that it was an opportunity to take care of her girls. Her subsequent divorce a year and one-half later, combined with the fact that her ex-husband stopped paying child support, meant that she was forced to survive of her own volition and abilities. She believes that when you are faced with a situation as drastic as losing half of the income from alimony, you realize that you're going to have to do whatever it takes to take care of your family.

## No External Financing

Pat has struggled financially since the beginning of her business. She never had external financing. Nobody would lend her money. Being divorced and from another country didn't help her. One banker asked, "What if you get homesick and then you leave?" At one point, Pat couldn't even rent space. So she put her savings, credit card, her daughters' college fund, and everything else she owned into the business. Pat says that if someone were to ask her to do that now, her response would be "no way!" There were weekends where she did not have enough money for Monday. She couldn't go to a bank or to her family because she didn't want to move back to Mexico. For the last contract she got, she went to a bank and the banker said, "No, this is too risky. We can't do it; I'm sorry." They didn't care that it was a contract for the government. They denied her the loan. Thankfully, the Small Business Administration did not feel the same way.

## SBA to the Rescue

Pat attended a seminar offered by the SBA to find out more about their loans for small businesses. Even though she was better informed, Pat did not pursue a loan from the SBA because someone had told her, "Nobody can get these loans because the paperwork is impossible; it's a joke." Then, when she returned to San Antonio from the seminar, her land lord wanted to raise her rent in the shopping center to almost $4,000 per month. Pat thought that was crazy, so once again, she took matters into her own hands and went looking for a building. She found a building and tried to get a bank loan, but as was said before, the bank thought investing in her was too risky. So with options running very low, Pat tried the SBA, and they approved a 504 loan. Fortunately, Pat was able to pay everything on time, building up her credit, enabling her to borrow whatever amount she needs now. But as they say, "When you need something, you can't have it, and when you don't need it, it's right there."

## No Easy Task

Pat was fortunate to have many great people help her become a successful entrepreneur since it is no easy task. Several mentors have helped her throughout her entrepreneurial career, and that is precisely what she is trying to do now: help other people. She believes there's no reason to struggle so much with trying to make a decent living and trying to develop your business. "If somebody could show you the proper route, you would get there faster," she says. She helps people because she feels blessed that great people helped her through the difficult years of her entrepreneurial formation. Even though her family still resides in Mexico, they are always in her thoughts. She remembers Sunday dinners when the conversation went something like, "Don't worry, I can help you with this or can I help you with that?" You need family to help each other and share the sad news or the good news. Pat had that all her life which is exactly what she is trying to provide for her children. Her daughter, Diana, graduated from Columbia University and now lives in New York City. While her second daughter, Lisa, gave Pat two beautiful grandchildren, Morgan and Patrick. Pat wants to help her daughters for as long as they need her. According to her, it is a part of life, "to be the wind beneath their wings, you help them fly."

## Advice

Pat's advice to aspiring entrepreneurs is to build a strong financial infrastructure. From the very beginning, try to pay off your loans as soon as possible so that if ever you need to do something else, you have a nest built up. According to her, that infrastructure will open doors to a lot of opportunities. Pat feels that she could have done better; she could have grown her company faster if she'd had the necessary capital to invest in the company, but it simply was not available. At certain points, she couldn't even advertise in the newspaper because she didn't have the money. But her luck changed. She also advises people to try to keep a clear head even in the face of seemingly insurmountable problems. For a long time she used to panic over issues, but now she doesn't; she can view things more clearly and solve problems faster.

## Exit Strategy

Pat would like to continue to head up Alamo Travel for many years to come. Once she's done there, she'd like to become a full-time volunteer and help people. According to Pat, Latinas have different problems; we're perceived differently. Pat thinks it is something to be proud of. "We have earned the respect of our community, the bankers, the government, because we have shown them that we are capable—*si se puede*," she says. For Pat, the most important accomplishment is that female entrepreneurs have gained national respect, a legacy that we are leaving to the women who will succeed us. A legacy of respect is the most valuable thing we can leave behind because we have shown the world that we can do it; we did it. Other women, not just Latinas, should have the same opportunities.

Pat was told that she couldn't do it, that she had an accent, that she would leave, that she was temperamental, that she was going to find a husband in the next six months, and that she was not going to pay attention to the business. But now Pat believes that Latinas finally have a place in the business world. Don't *you?*

# Chapter 5:

# Olga Martinez

President and CEO
Allright Diversified Services, Inc.
*www.allrightinc.com*

The often-cited phrase "small-town girl does good" has the name Olga Martinez written all over it. The fact that her firm's revenues reached $9.5 million in 2005 provides a glimpse of the success Olga has experienced. However, the facts and figures cannot convey the extent to which her success is not only a personal one but one for the farm-working community where she grew up-a small, rural town in the Central Valley of California.

According to Olga, residents of her community are not farm owners: they are THE farm workers. And she would know this, as she was one of them herself, along with her father, mother, and brothers. In fact, Olga comes from a long line of migrant farm workers. Her mother, who was born in Texas, has thirteen siblings, many of whom were migrant farm workers. Her father, who came from Mexico in 1958, was never able to master the English language because he was too busy working both day and night shifts as a farm worker.

Now in 2007, at seventy-seven years old and with limited English skills, he speaks about "pulling yourself up by the bootstraps to make your dreams come true." A number of Olga's relatives, who only speak Spanish, are still working both shifts as farm workers but they are happy to have the chance to do it, shares Olga. It was her father's love for America, gratitude to it, and belief in it, that encouraged her to reach for the stars. According to Olga, her father may not have mastered the English language, but he captured the spirit of what America is all about. He told her, "You can be anything you want to be, because *Mija,* this is America." Once he said to her, "If I had mastered the English language, I too would have had the opportunity to make someone of myself in this country." She replied, "You and mom should both be proud to have raised a family and given the limited resources you both had at the time; yet you both worked hard to make a better life for your kids." Her parents are still married and have been for almost fifty years. Olga is very proud of them.

## It Takes a Village

One cannot appreciate Olga's success without understanding her roots and what her success means to her and her community. Her soul has never left her community and her community has never left her. Everything Olga has done involves her friends and family. This is not a story about one woman making it on her own; it is about how she tapped into the heart, soul, and human resources of the community and created the extraordinary from the ordinary.

The rural town where she grew up in California has been referred to as the melon capital of the world. It was the climate years ago, before the unions protested, which caused the packing-shed owners to angrily pack in the fields rather than pay the union wages to pack in the sheds. Melon picking was one of the highest-paying jobs in agriculture in the 1970s and many young men and women, like Olga's parents, were thrilled to earn the $40 to $60 per day they earned as farm workers. Her hometown is about thirty-five miles from Fresno, California, on the west side of the San Joaquin Valley. It became productive farmland in the 1960s after federal and state water projects made irrigation water readily available.

Most of the farms grew very large and most grew cotton, melons, and increasingly, vegetables with the help of thousands of seasonal farm workers. The Central Valley Project Improvement Act of 1992, however, changed federal water policy and reduced the federal water available for west-side agriculture by 50 percent. As a result, land values have dropped by a significant percentage. The farm-worker towns in the area, like her rural hometown, began to suffer.

When she was only ten years old, Olga began to help her mother with her Avon business. That was her first foray into the world of business. Olga served as a ten-year-old bookkeeper, the inventory-control person, the manager, and her mother's all-around helper. She did such a good job that on Sundays, her mother put her and her brother on a Greyhound bus and sent her to her aunt to help her out with her hot-dog concession at another rural community's swap meet. Olga treasures those times of working with her aunt, as her aunt was killed by a drunk driver years later. It is through these experiences and later while working in her brother's construction business that she learned the basics of doing business. It was the only training she had in business before she started her own.

The town had experienced budget deficits, a nearly bankrupt school district, high unemployment in some months, bad water, and decaying housing. Olga had to be bused to Tranquility, California, an unincorporated town, to attend high school where she sat with the sons and daughters of farm owners for the first time. Over a decade ago, a study found that nearly half of her hometown's children lived in families with below-poverty-level incomes. This did not stop several thousand refugees of El Salvador's civil war from coming to her hometown to work in the fields, which added to the burden on the city's administration.

## A Field of Dreams

When Olga was thirteen years old, she began working in the fields. They were engaged in an agricultural process called *thinning* in which underbrush from the fields is cleared. It was back-breaking work according to Olga, the kind of work she was sure she was not going to do for the rest of her life. She decided at an early age that she was going to be a professional; she wanted to become an attorney. Despite having to work in the fields, when she visited her relatives in Mexico, she felt like a privileged American. Olga began to understand why her father loved America so much regardless of the difficult work he performed. He had also been engaged in back-breaking work in Mexico, but there, he only earned the equivalent of fifty cents per day for the same amount of hard labor.

Agriculture was the port of entry for Olga's father and many other immigrants from Mexico. Changes in both the U.S. and Mexico encouraged seasonal immigrant farm workers to settle in agricultural areas like her rural hometown, but these areas have typically had ill-defined and poorly financed economic-development strategies. Therefore, immigrants and their children had a hard time climbing up the U.S. job ladder. Nevertheless, the Martinez family was happy working in America. Olga's fortune changed for the better when she landed her first "indoor" job; she was fifteen years old when she got a job flipping hamburgers. At the time, she was just excited to be working indoors. Olga never imagined that one day, her family would own this hamburger business.

## Office Job

Olga received a boost in confidence after that. Later, she applied for an after-school job while in high school and was hired by a local seed company in Tranquility. They paid her minimum wage and taught her office skills that she was able to manage after school. Olga would take the late bus to go home in time to do homework. She continued to work there while she was sixteen and seventeen years old. Olga did so well that the office offered her full-time work during the summers. She learned how to work in an office environment for the first time in her life, and was exposed to working with people of non-minority descent. Some of them were daughters of farmers, and Olga found that hearing their point of view of life was interesting. She remembers one of the bosses asking her why Hispanics vote for Democrats as a block. She could not answer that, given she was not eligible to vote. She could only respond that, "If one family does something and likes it, then the rest of the families do it as well."

## Flipping Burgers and Her Life Around

Who would have thought that a little job like flipping hamburgers could lead to the transformation of the socioeconomic status of one farm-worker family? After she had worked in the hamburger business for two years, the owner approached her and persuaded her to ask her parents to purchase the business. This was a big step for her parents; they never thought about going into business and knew nothing about that kind of business. Yet, their little daughter was persuasive, so much so that she was able to talk them into mortgaging their only asset, their tiny home, to purchase the hamburger business. From that point, the family's destiny changed and they went from farm workers to business owners. Olga was only nineteen at the time. Her mentoring of others started at that age; her first protégés were her parents. She was nervous but knew that it was the only ticket out of the fields for her family. For that, she was willing to do whatever it took to give her parents the dream of having their own business in the United States.

Olga is the eldest child and while her parents did not pressure her to help them transform their lives, she pressured herself to make a difference in their lives. Her parents listened to her because she was a serious child. In fact, Olga shouldered so much responsibility in the family that she said she felt like "an adult in a child's body." From helping care for her three brothers to working in the fields and the hamburger place to helping out her mother and aunts with their side businesses, Olga shouldered great responsibility since she was a child.

## A Dream Deferred

To become a professional, Olga needed to attend a university and her parents did not support that idea. At the age of seventeen, she wanted to attend UCLA to experience living away from home. As part of a strict Hispanic family, under no circumstances could she leave home.

Olga attended California State University, Fresno. Her parents made arrangements with an uncle and aunt for Olga to stay at their home during the week in Fresno, which is only about forty-five minutes away from her hometown, but she had to come home every weekend. Due to this restriction, Olga had little or no social life.

According to Olga, her parents continued to be strict. They developed a program of school to an after school job to studying after work. Olga says, "My life consisted of driving the family car at age seventeen to the university, *an hour drive,* going shopping to purchase the supplies for the hamburger business during my break time while in Fresno, driving an hour back home to work in the hamburger business, then studying before I went to sleep. I was seventeen years old when I started college and I was already tired— but I wasn't too tired to purchase another business, however."

When asked why she chose to study Environmental Health Sciences, she replied, "I thought it would be more interesting to be the health inspector at restaurants than just to be inspected as was our fast food on an annual basis, given the county laws. It taught me how to better operate my family's business." It wasn't until later in her own construction business that the Environmental Sciences education would be helpful. The education also assisted her in landing a temporary job working for the Department of Health Services for the State of California at twenty years old. She worked for the health department full-time, assisted in running the family business, and attended college. It was a busy time for Olga during her early twenties.

## Sacrifices

When Olga graduated from California State University, Fresno in 1982 with a B.S., her family still owned the fast-food business and by this time, everyone in the family was involved. Olga branched out and began to purchase what she calls fixer-uppers. The business was successful and her family started a savings account and was able to pay off their second mortgage which they borrowed to use as a down payment for the business. Because Olga, her parents, and brothers all had full-time jobs and worked the business after their regular job and on their days off, they were able to save some money. They sacrificed quite a bit as they did not celebrate birthdays and holidays together like other families since the fast-food restaurant remained open seven days per week. Someone was always missing from the family, as they were busy running the business.

Coming from her small rural town, she didn't know anyone who knew anything about stocks and bonds or other investment options, so with her mother's encouragement, she bought more and more fixer-uppers. Olga eventually purchased a second restaurant in 1984, a Mexican Taqueria. Olga, being the entrepreneur that she was, did not know how to cook; but, she says, she knew how to eat. So she kept interviewing people until she found a great, honest cook. Olga says, "Only in America can you do something so crazy as open a restaurant even if you do not know any recipes, much less how to cook." It is courage that kept her going and trying different ventures.

By this time, Olga began to understand what it was like to be a businesswoman. Her first big purchase was a brand-new 1986 BMW. Many were amazed, "I was a small-town businesswoman—I had the 'right' car, a family business with two restaurants, and I was wearing a size six-to-eight; I was hot to trot."

## Trotting Off to the Big City

Like any retail business, her restaurants required 24/7 involvement, she was tired and wasn't having any fun. Olga's parents were trying to keep her focused, but she looked for any excuse to escape. It was time to see the world; at age twenty-seven she had only seen her rural hometown, Fresno, and Mexico. After selling the second restaurant, she moved to Los Angeles. While there, Olga worked for a consulting firm that helped small businesses increase their productivity. Once she'd lived in Los Angeles, she felt she had fully experienced the big-city life. But along the way, she got engaged and moved back to Fresno because she realized, "There's no place like home."

Unfortunately, Olga's marriage did not work out and she divorced after a short time. In looking back, she felt as if the traditional Hispanic family pressure was the reason to get married even though she had not had time to date very much. Olga later realized and shares with young girls, that it doesn't matter if your family feels it is time for you to marry; do not marry unless you are ready.

## Back to Business

According to Olga, she was never very interested in dating; her excitement came from work and volunteering for good causes. She explains, "Give me a business or a cause to run, and I'm happy." So her brother, who owned a construction firm, gave her his business to run. It was in the early '90s and she was once again free to devote herself fully to helping her brother in his business. Olga did all of his administration work out of her house in Fresno, CA. He had previously focused on plumbing and roofing, but when Olga got her hands on the business, she encouraged him to broaden his scope and start remodeling homes for the local housing authority and to obtain his general-contracting license.

After finding that she liked the construction industry, Olga wanted to help her brother grow his construction business. Always the risk-taker, she started taking risks in his name; sometimes he didn't even know what they were contracted to perform until they were about to start. As a result, Olga's brother considered firing her many times. One time she landed a $114,000 job with the local housing authority. Since she knew her brother would say no, she hired another crew to perform the job. Once he got over it and forgave her, he told her to market to the housing authority some more. Marketing the firm was her forte; Olga marketed the firm so aggressively people thought she owned it. Olga says, "Once you get on a roll and find out that you are an effective multitasker, there is no stopping you, and you begin to look for new challenges." Consequently, in 1998 Olga decided to start her *own* construction business, as she wanted to conquer the world whereas her brother wanted to conquer the small communities. It wasn't a challenge for Olga to only conquer a radius of fifty miles. Her vision was to "aim for the stars and the moon."

## Constructing a New Business

In order to finance her business, Olga sold everything she owned, including her house, with the exception of her now twelve-year-old BMW. She even sold her purebred kittens. Olga owned a very rare cat she had received as a gift, whose kittens fetched upward of $300 each. When she told her nine-year-old niece how she got started, that she had to sell the kittens for money, her niece was horrified. Today's joke is that Olga sold everything except her mama cat and an old BMW to get her business started.

Olga's decision to start a business was not made before consulting with friends and associates. She asked them what she should do and they advised her to do something with the federal government. Olga wasn't sure if the federal government would hire her because she had no track record. And sure enough, when she did start her firm and marketed to the federal government, a lot of doors were slammed in her face. Yes, they knew she worked for her brother but she had no actual experience in her own company's name. The only experience she could offer was as a management consultant, which was not a service the federal government purchased at that time. Though she started her company in 1998, she did not get serious about construction services until the year 2000 when she obtained her contractor's license. She now had the license to ask for work in the construction services, even with no experience. She had to convince the government to give her a chance and to trust her to do an exceptional job. She finally prevailed.

It took two years before Olga landed her first U.S. Government contract. In the first year, her sales totaled $30,000 all from consulting services. It wasn't until 2000 when she received her first contract to upgrade a Hypochlorite Generating System in the desert for the Navy that things began to turn around. The contract award was for $129,000, but Olga never would have been awarded that assignment if she hadn't had the foresight to get certified with the U.S. Small Business Administration as a minority- and woman-owned 8(a) firm.

This program only gives you the opportunity to negotiate with the federal government; however, there is no guarantee that you will ever get a contract. There are many 8(a) companies in the country that have never received a government contract. It takes hard work, dedication, and self-marketing.

## Performing Government Services

Federal government procurement is complex. There are laws, regulations, procedures, and preference programs that determine the degrees of preferential access to contracts for different socioeconomic groups. The U.S. Small Business Administration (SBA) plays an important role in leveling the playing field for small firms and for minority-owned firms by serving as their advocate through negotiating prime and subcontract goals for various small-business categories. The SBA ensures that cumulative goals for all agencies meet or exceed a government-wide 23-percent small-business total. Toward this end, SBA compiles and analyzes agencies' achievements against their individual goals and reports the results to the President of the United States.

What does it mean to have an 8(a) certification? In a nutshell: a lot. Regulations permit 8(a) companies to form beneficial partnerships and allow federal agencies to streamline the contracting process. Participation in the 8(a) program is divided into two phases over nine years: a four-year developmental stage and a five-year transition stage. In fiscal year 1998, more than 6,100 firms participated in the 8(a) program and were awarded $6.4 billion in federal contract awards. Benefits of the program include: Participants can receive sole-source contracts, up to a ceiling of $3.5 million for goods and services and $5 million for manufacturing. SBA has signed Memorandums of Understanding (MOU) with twenty-five federal agencies, allowing them to contract directly with certified 8(a) firms, and, 8(a) firms are permitted to form joint ventures and teams to bid on contracts This enhances the ability of 8(a) firms to perform larger prime contracts and overcome the effects of contract bundling, the combining of two or more contracts together into one large contract. One aspect of the program to understand, however, is that it is not a hand-out program. One has to deliver presentations, have bonding which is tough to acquire, and convince the government that she can perform an excellent job. One must prove oneself, as there are many 8(a) companies and obtaining contracts is not a certainty. Many, many 8(a) firms never obtain sole-source contracts from the government. Olga worked hard at satisfying the government, even if it meant her being on the job at times.

## A Key Benefit of the 8(a) Program

The U.S. Small Business Administration's Mentor-Protégé program enhances the capability of 8(a) participants to compete more successfully for federal-government contracts. The program encourages private-sector relationships and expands SBA's efforts to identify and respond to the developmental needs of 8(a) clients. Mentors provide technical and management assistance, financial assistance in the form of equity investments and/or loans, subcontract support, and assistance in performing prime contracts through joint-venture arrangements with 8(a) firms.

Olga has benefited from the 8(a) Mentor-Protégé program and her success in the program is a classic example of the goals the program has sought to achieve. It is a win-win for all concerned—for Olga, her mentor, the client, and ultimately, the nation—when firms like Olga's are empowered and thus able to contribute more to the tax base and to employ workers. Olga acknowledges that the timing was auspicious for the start of her new business because it coincided with the SBA's launch of its Mentor-Protégé program. Olga had just returned from Washington, D.C., and shared information about the program with a local 8(a) firm about to graduate. She then convinced the owner to take on her company. It was agreed upon and continued for several years that turned out to be beneficial for both companies.

## A Perfect Match

From the very beginning, Olga never sought to do business solely on her own. She started out in a family business and she remains in one, but the family has grown and connotes a broader meaning of family: the *community* family. Her new family included a nonprofit/for-profit organization committed to economic development in East Los Angeles. The President/CEO gave her an opportunity to work as a consultant in order to continue to expand his organization into other segments. There was a synergy there from the beginning: Olga started out refurbishing dilapidated homes, while this organization also built homes, albeit on a much grander scale. Established in 1968, this organization has grown phenomenally. From the building of affordable homes to lending of millions of dollars to families and small-business entrepreneurs, this organization's business philosophy, like Olga's, is inseparable from its social philosophy.

Olga met the President/CEO of this large organization during a business dinner at a convention in San Francisco in 1997. She remembers that she had to change into her evening clothes in her car because she and her girlfriend with whom she had driven from Fresno could not afford a hotel room. Nevertheless, she was able to convince him to hire her as a consultant. That made for an interesting arrangement because he was also a mentor and she was his consultant.

This organization along with her local SBA mentor also from Fresno would later become the wind beneath Allright Diversified's sails. But Olga was completely in charge in one of her first sales; the Navy had asked her to cut their lawns. Olga replied, "Sure! There is no job too big or too small." She then gathered resources within her community and got a crew together to cut the lawns. She had to be very creative, as she did not own any commercial lawn mowers. The contract continued for several years, only it grew into a much larger one. In fact, at one point in 2004–2005, Olga was about to negotiate to mow the lawns for the IRS, which had a very large facility in Fresno that they wanted her company to maintain. Olga recalls, "We were looking at mowing their lawns, pruning their trees, and performing other landscape-related functions that would have required a four-man crew for forty hours per week; however, the government could not meet the budget required to perform such duties."

## Lessons Learned

If you are going to be involved in federal-government contracting, you have to get out and walk the halls to figure out who is who and what is what in Washington, D.C. Fortunately, Olga began doing that early on while she was consulting for her client. The President/CEO allowed her to accompany him to market his firm. In the process, she learned a number of things about how to operate in government contracting.

One thing that Olga found important was to learn how to use the small-business facilitation resources in the federal government. One resource, the Business Opportunity Specialist (BOS) of the SBA, was a valuable resource for her, as she was simultaneously learning about the government and how to do business at the same time. Not having studied business at her university, Olga had to learn on the job. Her BOS made the job easier by conducting many workshops on all aspects of running a business. She laments that with downsizing, SBA has retired many experienced BOSs and their replacements are just learning the 8(a) program and how to be of assistance themselves. Being able to access business-development services is important for young firms like Olga's. She notes, "I had to learn from the college of hard knocks!" Several years later, Olga began to understand for the first time all aspects of doing business, such as cash-flow projections, work-in-progress (WIP) reports and all the other financial statements one must provide to the bank. She says, "These are the things that my SBA mentor did for me, and now my staff and I have to do them for my company."

Unfortunately, Olga has also been disappointed by the small-business representatives she has encountered in the federal-government agencies, noting that many of them are political appointees who take four years to learn the agencies and by the time they learn, it is time for them to leave office. It is unfortunate because "They are learning on your time while your clock is ticking." Walking the halls is not just about meeting people; it also entails doing one's homework to learn the rules. The key to federal-government procurement is the Federal Acquisition Regulations, which is a complex, dense code of rules and regulations about government contracting. The more you know about this, the better.

## By the Book

Another important lesson Olga has learned about working with the government is that you have to heed all of the rules, regulations, and administrative requirements. It is not like when you run a family business. According to Olga, when she worked for her brother, they were loose in their administration and procedures. Now all of that has changed; you must become a more professional business versus a mom-and-pop with no manuals or rules.

It is something Olga and her brother are now working through as she begins to mentor him in performing federal-government work. It had always been her dream to reconnect with her brother and his construction firm. In the past, they went their separate ways due in part to sibling rivalry and in part to the fact that Olga's brother was solely focused on the private sector. Finally, in 2007, her brother decided that perhaps it is not a bad thing to work for the federal government and now she has an opportunity to mentor him and reciprocate for having been given her first job in the construction industry.

## It Is "Allright" to Be Diversified

Olga had a vision when she chose the name for her firm; she knew she would diversify and grow and that is what she has done. Though she must admit, she borrowed the name "Allright" from her brother, as his company is called "Allright" too. She has asked for forgiveness and he has since forgiven her. His company is called "Allright Construction" and her company is "Allright Diversified Services Inc." So far, her biggest contract was for $3 million to build a 20,000-square-foot facility for the National Guard. She leveraged her relationship with her SBA mentor to win and perform the assignment and leveraged it to win contracts with the Air Force, Department of Labor, Army, Navy, NASA, National Park, Veterans Administration, National Guard, and others. In addition to working with her SBA mentor, an 8(a) graduate, Olga has also worked with other strategic partners to whom she credits her success. She is grateful and thankful to her two mentors and strategic partners for their support and contribution. She wants them to know that they will be making a major contribution to other small-business owners in the near future, through their previous, current, and future mentorship of her business.

## Constructing the Road Ahead

According to Olga, she is very concerned about maintaining a profitable business in the state of California and she needs to be mindful of watching the business. Health insurance, bonding, and workman's compensation are critical to make-or-break issues and in the case of Olga's industry, bonding is very tough to acquire as it requires lots of working capital within a company to obtain bonding. Despite this difficulty, bonding is required by the federal government for construction projects. While most of Olga's concern is focused on issues within the state of California, there are external factors that also have a bearing on her performance. For instance, the Iraq situation has had a direct impact upon Olga's firm and upon her as a human being.

Sometimes the agencies will ask for emergency jobs to be performed, given troops are leaving and returning from the war. This is her way of serving her country—by providing the federal agencies immediate, urgent services to better assist the troops. Olga takes great pride in doing so, in part because she had a part-time assistant who was deployed for three years during the Iraq war with only four days' notice.

Olga wants to mentor other small emerging businesses to become an 8(a) success, or successful veteran or service disabled-veteran companies. She is now making available her nine years of experience to other companies. She constantly reminds herself to empower others rather than to give a handout. It is best to teach someone how to fish, rather than give them a fish, she believes. Olga is also looking at possibly investing in firms to assist them in growing. This plan is in the future once she has formulated a financially sound business plan.

In the future, Olga also wants to penetrate the international market. Early on, she tried to convince her strategic partners and mentors to support her in targeting the international market, but they pulled her back to reality. They told her to conquer her own state first—in fact, they advised Olga to focus exclusively on Northern California, but at least she prevailed in having them agree to target all of California.

As the federal government is an ever-changing marketplace, there is a need to stay current and to change with the times. Olga says, "Recently, I have been advised to get a GSA Schedule because work in my industry is now being contracted through the schedule. This is new; previously, construction work was never contracted through the schedule." The need to obtain additional certifications is seemingly endless, but work is not everything in life.

## Creating a Balance

Marriage is not in Olga's plans right now. Olga states she is glad that her whole family is supporting each other and, right or wrong, they discuss business all the time. They try to not talk shop when it is family time, but it is in their blood by now. Their father works with her brother, and her other brother works with them too. Olga is also assisting her mother in raising a now thirteen-year-old god-child. As for community involvement, it remains a constant in her life. However, she says she has to become smarter about it in the future and remember to always watch the store. Olga's company did not grow faster sooner because she was too involved with the community. Olga is a community person; she enjoys giving back. One of the things that brings her joy is sitting down with other business owners to share what has and has not worked for her development. Olga also gives back to her relatives in Mexico and has helped to financially support her grandmother, who died a few years ago at the age of ninety-eight.

"Now that Allright Diversified Services, Inc., has its bonding and that I know all aspects of running a business, I can say that I am 100 percent a real businesswoman." It doesn't get more professional than that.

## The Unexpected

Olga experienced the most horrific experience of her life, when she suffered a ruptured brain aneurysm that required emergency brain surgery on June 18, 2006. After going from her local clinic to the ER by ambulance where she received a CT scan, she was told that her brain was bleeding due to a ruptured brain aneurysm and she needed emergency brain surgery that could possibly be fatal. The doctors had to call at least six hospitals to see who had a surgeon available. The surgery took place at the University of California Davis, where Olga was flown by helicopter not knowing if her family would ever see her alive again. This was the only hospital that had a surgeon available and a bed in the Intensive Care Unit (ICU). Olga remained in the ICU for approximately two weeks. Her family was elated and thankful to God that she survived. After that, she was discharged into her family's care.

Olga and I are very close friends and when I was informed about the events, I could not believe it. She had come to visit me in Los Angeles a few days before the surgery. A group of friends and I all prayed to give her the strength to survive these difficult moments in her life, and we are thoroughly grateful that she did.

Once at home, she began to read about brain aneurysms and finally realized the severity of what had happened to her. It is unknown as to why human beings get brain aneurysms, though doctors say it could be one of three causes: high blood pressure, genetics , or an earlier untreated head injury. Olga had none of these. How serious and dangerous this medical condition could have been! For a month after she was discharged, she was frightened of going to sleep for fear of not waking up. Olga had a completely different appreciation for life in an ICU hospital bed after closing the chapter on her hospital stay by returning for a visit months after her release.

Thankfully a friend told her about a church in Madera, California, called Face to Face Ministries under the leadership of Pastor David Morgan, where Olga states that she "accepted Jesus as her savior like never before." As her spiritual healing increases, her medical healing is miraculously improving. She also was rid of the depression that comes with a major surgery. Her friends, family, and new spiritual family all assisted her in her healing, spiritually, emotionally, medically, and financially. Olga thanks her "Almighty God for giving her a second chance," and does not take life for granted.

Her family cancelled the purchase of Olga's new home while in the hospital, given they did not know if they were going to have to make funeral arrangements, let alone deal with escrow of a new home. Thankfully, she is back at her company, Allright Diversified Services, and has closed escrow on a beautiful house which was a better deal given the market change. She appreciates her brother stepping into her company after her medical emergency. Olga's new mission is to make a difference in people's lives. Today, she and her surgeon are discussing starting a foundation to fund more research so the world knows how to prevent and treat brain aneurysms. It is a passionate cause of Olga's and one on which she is working diligently. She is stabilizing her company to give her the time to start her foundation which will lead to making presentations to the Bill and Melinda Gates Foundations of the world and to Congress for support. Her dream is to travel with her surgeon throughout the world to impart this knowledge and educate others. Her surgeon, Dr. John Chang, whom she is very thankful to for saving her life through his gift from GOD, will share with other medical professionals while Olga shares with the public, the results acquired from the foundation's research. Stay tuned, as many miraculous events shall take place while this thriving Latina entrepreneur, Olga Martinez, continues her commitment to save many lives through her experience and by working with others who are also committed to her vision.

# Chapter 6:

# Theresa Alfaro Daytner

CEO/President
Daytner Construction Group
*www.daytnercorp.com*

What do the construction industry and six children have in common? The answer: Theresa Alfaro Daytner, a woman who has embraced everything she was given to come out on top. Theresa has always possessed an entrepreneurial spirit that has propelled her to a success that at one time, she could only have imagined.

Born in Takoma Park, Maryland, Theresa comes from a diverse background. She is a second-generation South American on her father's side. Her mother was adopted and is believed to be of Irish decent. Her paternal grandparents hailed from Venezuela and Chile. One of Theresa's grandfathers spoke no English and worked as a window washer at the Ritz Tower Hotel on Park Avenue in Manhattan. Since her grandfather didn't understand English, his children were forbidden from speaking anything but Spanish in their home. Although her father was born in New York, he didn't learn to speak English until he started elementary school and needed to communicate outside of his home.

Theresa's father, Blas, was born in The Bronx, New York, during the Great Depression in 1929. His family was forced to move frequently from apartment to apartment at a time when the first month's rent was free for new tenants. At one time, when he was fourteen, Blas landed a job as a dishwasher and began making more money than his father, so the elder patriarch made Blas quit. Machismo at its finest, her grandfather was a strict disciplinarian and a fiercely proud man.

Growing up, Theresa's family lived in a townhouse where her parents hosted great parties with lots of music, laughter, and dancing. There were many cultural influences in her family life. Theresa recalls a particular incident that opened her eyes to her unique situation; she realized that although she looks Irish, she feels Latina. She says, "I can't tell you how disappointed I was to go to my first high school party in suburban Maryland. Stupid drinking games and sitting or standing around were not my idea of a party. Where was the dancing? This was one of the first times I realized that I may *look* like my peers, but I was very different from them. This had everything to do with my Hispanic cultural experience, but also with where my father had come from ... the ghetto." There weren't many Hispanics in Greenbelt, Maryland; even now, Mexicans think her family is Puerto Rican and Anglo-Americans think they're Mexican.

Anxious to see more of the world, Theresa married her first boyfriend at nineteen, about a week before turning twenty. She didn't get any farther than Nebraska. Theresa started and stopped her college career several times. One particular turning point for her occurred when she was living in Lincoln, Nebraska. She felt like she was the only person in the state with black hair! Even worse was the fact that women had little in the way of career options or systems of support. That was two strikes against her.

She was twenty and working full-time for minimum wage in a hospital cafeteria. This was not what she had envisioned for herself as a young girl, so she went back to the East Coast and enrolled at the University of Maryland at College Park. Theresa was not about to stop until she had received a diploma. Although she didn't care much for accounting, she was determined to acquire a marketable skill. School was not her favorite place to be, but if she was taking classes, she wasn't earning money, so school was an investment that needed to pay off. Ultimately, she was the first person from her father's family to graduate college, albeit at the age of twenty-five with a one-year-old in tow.

## Always an Entrepreneur

Theresa's father started so many businesses that Theresa doesn't even remember all of them. She does, however, recall him having kind of a "get rich quick" mentality with his businesses. Looking back, she believes this is what helped her to focus more on building her own businesses. She took note of his mistakes, but also his willingness to take risks. Theresa's risks are much more calculated and are coupled with a belief that the world will not end if one of these ventures fails to bear fruit. She believes you move on and as long as you have your family, all the rest falls into place.

Theresa wanted to be an entrepreneur ever since she was a little girl; she just didn't know what business she would create. Although she took the long road, she eventually decided to study accounting in preparation for being a business owner. She says, "They just didn't offer those sexy entrepreneurial programs back in the day." Even though Theresa struggled with the idea of sitting still, "focusing and being with some pretty boring people who actually like that stuff," it sure did wonders for her credibility.

At some point, her husband was working as a roofer and she convinced him that they could start their own roofing business. From what she saw, his friends were doing it and making great money. If she added a professional attitude to dealing with clients, and if they showed up when they said they would, they'd be on their way. Theresa started her first business, a residential roofing company, while still in college in 1988.

Studying accounting paid off, as Theresa received five job offers the semester before she graduated college. By December 1988, she had accepted an offer to start working at a highly respected Washington, D.C., regional CPA firm. She graduated in May 1989, worked throughout that summer at her roofing business, and then began full-time work as a professional in the city.

She left the marriage and the roofing company in 1990, with a two-year-old, an accounting degree, and start-up experience in her portfolio.

The year 1990 was a pivotal one for Theresa. With a bad marriage behind her, and facing life as a single mother, Theresa chose to leave her position as a staff accountant at a Washington, D.C., CPA firm to take what she calls a "paycheck" job that was close to home and would require no more than forty hours a week.

Theresa's mother had recently been diagnosed with multiple sclerosis and her father, with very aggressive prostate cancer. This would be Theresa's first experience with the notion that "what didn't kill her, made her stronger!"

Theresa then started a job as a project accountant on large commercial construction projects for a well-respected regional general contractor. This is where she met her second husband, Allen. During this time Theresa took and passed the CPA exam the first time around! Then, her next business opportunity came to life and she decided to open her own consulting, accounting, and tax practice.

Theresa built the practice and advised other would-be entrepreneurs on how to create a business plan, keep the books, think strategically, and so on. She made her own work schedule and was sure to take summers off with her kids. Theresa remarried in 1994. By 1997, she had moved her office into her home to be closer to her children, three daughters by then and her ailing parents, and had made arrangements for childcare to visit her house. Thankfully, her parents helped out where they could. Mom sat and held the new baby, while Dad cooked and helped chauffer.

Her new husband, Allen, brought a daughter, Alysha, to the marriage, so they started their family with two daughters. When Allen and Theresa started dating in 1990, Alysha was four years old and Katherine was two. Michelle was born a year after they married, in 1995 and Candice arrived in 1997.

By 2000, Theresa was bored with accounting. Furthermore, it was always her intent that accounting would be nothing more than a stepping stone for her next business and she was anxious to get a fresh start with something new. She got something new, but it was not exactly what she had in mind. She and her husband found out they were going to have another baby and, as they soon discovered, they would be expecting twins, adding two boys to their four girls. Theresa shut down the accounting practice and shuffled clients along to CPA friends.

For Theresa, 2001 was a blur. Her father had developed cancer that required chemotherapy and her mother's disease continued to progress, all while they tried to be good parents to the older kids, the pre-schoolers and care for the babies. Once she could breathe again, she decided it would be a great time to start a new business! Her husband had been an employee his whole life and Theresa knew he would have to be coached and reassured that they would be able to handle such responsibility. She eventually convinced him that starting their own business was a worthwhile endeavor.

Theresa started Daytner Construction Group, a construction management and consulting company in 2003. She had started exploring a niche market years ago and did significant research into the industry and its trends prior to this decision. This research process revealed that their particular strength was a combination of her business experience and vision coupled with her husband's experience, work ethic, and reputation in performing construction management. This gave the "team" both the managerial and technical expertise necessary to launch and grow a successful venture. Since she had been planning for a lifetime and basically "scheming" to get her husband involved, once she had him on board, they started the business. Theresa started the company in January, and her husband joined her full time in March of 2003.

In the first year of business, Theresa attended a conference in Washington, D.C., and instantly gravitated toward the Latino group in the room. They laughed, danced, and got to know each other. At first, Theresa was unaware what a talented group of accomplished businesspeople she was surrounded by. These women became instant role models for her and she couldn't get enough of their stories and insight.

She realized that her own dreams weren't crazy and that she wouldn't have to sell herself short or become someone else to make those dreams a reality. These were actually very nice, normal people like Theresa.

Theresa and her husband worked on a business plan together and have continued to fine-tune it as additional experience makes them rethink things. They first started finding customers in the people they knew. They told everyone what they were doing and while he kept tabs on his existing contacts, Theresa went out to find new customers and new opportunities. The majority of their customers were acquired through word-of-mouth.

## Financing

As for the financing of her business, Theresa did it "the same way as everyone else: credit cards and home equity." Thankfully, the housing market brought some instant equity. Theresa has been fortunate to establish a very good banking relationship and that helped them obtain money when they really didn't have anything more than a strong belief that things were going to work out.

All along, she has believed that it wasn't a matter of "if" her business would be successful, but "when." With that in mind, along with her accounting background, Theresa has always considered cash flow to be either her best friend or worst enemy. In seeking business financing, her goal has always been to make sure she can say 'yes' to new contracts without worrying about how to make that first sixty or so days of payroll, or get laptops and cell phones in the hands of project managers from day one.

All the drudgery of studying accounting and keeping track of the books for other small-business owners was now paying off. This background gave her instant credibility and the right tools and vocabulary to ask for the money necessary to finance her business.

## Obstacles

Theresa has always had young children when she started a new business. So, the main obstacle for Theresa was always juggling money and babies. She's always been very fortunate to have an incredible support system in her family. At a moment's notice, her sister would babysit for Theresa's children while watching three of her own, while her father would shuttle them all around.

The first three years of the business were slow and money was very tight. In fact, they're still paying themselves back for the home equity and credit-card "loans" that kept them afloat during that time. Theresa's dad, lovingly known to family as Papi, passed away, and her mother and children needed her, so she did not have a full-time commitment to growing the business, although she continued to develop relationships that would serve them well down the road.

Besides her own personal struggles of being the primary care-giver for those she loves and feeling the undeniable call to be an entrepreneur, she continues to encounter the inevitable stereotype that comes with being a woman in construction and working with her husband. According to Theresa, "It seems to be a given in this society that either a) my husband put me up to this and I must be a 'front,' or b) that this was my husband's idea and I "keep the books" for *his* business." Nothing could be farther from the truth.

## Certifications

They did not need any certifications in the beginning. Now they know that they would not be able to get into certain markets, like those of open exchange with the federal government, without having a certification to leverage against the "big boys" in their field. Now that they have obtained an SBA 8(a) certification, they are starting to do business with the federal government, but are careful in choosing a company to mentor them as they grow in that target market.

After realizing the value of these certifications in the marketplace and especially with potential teaming partners, they have obtained additional certifications as woman-owned, and minority-owned in different jurisdictions, including state and local governments.

Theresa states, "We had heard, and now know it's true, that the certifications are merely hunting licenses and you have to learn how to market them to potential customers and large companies with subcontracting goals."

Theresa's father died on October 3, 2004. Her business remained in limbo after her father's passing and she knew she was "stuck." A change of scenery was much needed, so she packed up four of the younger kids and headed to her brother's ranch in Idaho to clear her head. Theresa returned invigorated and ready to push forward. That was the summer of 2005. Flash forward to the end of 2006: Their revenue had grown 800 percent from the previous year. With renewed commitment, Theresa stepped on the gas and never looked back! This year they expect to pass the $1 million revenue threshold and anticipate another sharp-growth year.

## Mentors

Theresa listens to anyone who will share and tries to surround herself with people whom she admires. That said, she's always had mentors, and two early ones were Olga Martinez of Allright Diversified Services and Ricardo Martinez of Project Enhancement

Corporation. Theresa looks up to both of these fine people and hopes to share her experience with someone the way they have with her. She is not afraid to ask for help or advice from anyone, and this has proven very useful in finding mentors.

## Support

Theresa's team has periodic business meetings with an "open book" approach to developing the business. She is in the process of creating an advisory board to meet about twice annually to review and revise vision, mission, and strategy.

There is a business coach with whom Theresa works, along with participating in an executive business roundtable organization called Vistage. It's a phenomenal program with great speakers, incredible support, and valuable exposure to topics and peer experience not found elsewhere.

## Cultural Differences

Theresa has a unique perspective because she looks more Irish than Latina. Always interesting are the things she hears people say— things they wouldn't say if she fit their stereotypical image of a Latina. For the most part, Theresa is respected by the people with whom she works. As a Latina and a woman in the construction world, especially in business development, Theresa has learned that it doesn't hurt to stand out in a crowd. She also finds it interesting, and not a bad thing, that it is now quite fashionable to speak another language. We're ahead of the curve in speaking more than one language AND understanding another culture.

## The Balancing Act

Theresa is often asked how she balances her personal and business life. The truth is, sometimes she feels good at it and sometimes she doesn't. The key is to pay attention to those gut feelings and always be willing to make adjustments. She has an extraordinary support system. Theresa and her husband are true life partners, whether in raising children or growing a business.

This is what she likes best about having her own business and being a mom: being her own boss. Theresa gets to set the rules according to her priorities. The added bonus is that now she gets to create a family-friendly environment for her employees. That really fuels her when she thinks about how big she wants her business to be in the future.

Latina entrepreneurs have the opportunity to become successful on their terms. Not only are they in a position to create jobs in this country, but they can choose to improve the quality of life for workers. In fact, she is not personally motivated to make lots of money just to be well off, but also to use economic empowerment in finding a voice in the American political system and supporting community programs that she believes in, that positively impact people's lives.

## Accomplishments

Theresa thinks big. She is very proud of that because it comes naturally; she doesn't know any other way to think. This frame of mind is possessed by all of the women business leaders she encounters. Theresa recently competed in and won a business contest called "Make Mine a Million" (M3). What an awesome program to get women business owners thinking about scaling up their businesses! Daily, the program is planting the seeds of possibility in people's minds and creating role models. What vision from the founder of Count Me In, Nell Merlino, and the M3 Premier Sponsor, Susan Sobbott, President of OPEN by American Express.

Theresa also likes to bring her kids to business functions when she can. That's not very often, but she enjoys being a role model for other women and for her daughters. She tries to share experiences with her children, like when she's nominated for an award. This is a great opportunity to let them experience what it's all about.

## Future

Theresa says, "Looking back, we were nuts!" Since it was agreed that she and her husband were employable, the worst-case scenario was that if things didn't work out with their business, someone would have to get an outside paycheck.

Currently, Theresa is tightening up her team and strengthening areas that require improvement in order to scale up the business. They are currently negotiating with an engineering firm to mentor them in the federal-contracting arena and look forward to a rewarding and long-term relationship. At this point, the company has almost eight years left in the SBA 8(a) program and they'd like to maximize their potential in this market, especially with all the domestic military building programs taking place in the next several years.

The company is currently being split into two divisions. Besides targeting the federal government as a client, they will continue to establish their niche and reputation in serving as an Owner's Representative on the private/commercial sector. When funds permit, they would like to venture into real-estate development and create a steady stream of residual and passive income from commercial leases, while growing their portfolio.

Ultimately, Theresa and her husband would like to have a well-defined exit strategy in about ten years.

Her personal future aspirations are to have enough money to travel the world when and where she chooses. She says, "I don't need much, but I would definitely like to create a legacy of wealth that will be passed on to my heirs, like college funds and down payments for first houses and such. Like most of my sister Latina entrepreneurs, we don't know this model, but are willing to learn it!"

Theresa was not afraid of taking risks, but she was afraid of failing and sometimes, even afraid of success. She had never known anyone who was wildly successful in business the way she wanted to be; however, Theresa has always been motivated by the idea that she could create her own destiny. She is also motivated and inspired by friends who have gone down this path successfully. And, she is motivated to reward those who have contributed to her entrepreneurial dream, including family and employees. In the end, according to Theresa, here is what matters: "Laugh often, live every day with thanks in your heart, be a good person, do the right thing. Do this, and you'll sleep better at night and look forward to each new day's adventure!"

## Advice

"It's tough to have the answers on how to do all these things well and even harder to give advice to another woman who wants to have a rich and full life comprised of both 'raising' a business and raising a family. I've heard other women recommend that we stop trying to do it all at the same time; I would agree that this advice makes sense, but you also have to 'make hay when the sun is shining.'" Theresa has been impatient but passionate about pursuing her own entrepreneurial dreams. She doesn't feel that anyone could have convinced her to do things differently. But, it would definitely be easier on everyone if she had taken on these challenges one at a time. One could go to college; have a career; and start, grow, and sell a business before ever having children or one could have kids young, stay home with them, and start a business when they're all in school full time. Each one has its own appeal, according to Theresa.

"So, life is a marathon, not a sprint. Don't try to do it all at once like me. You'll probably breathe better and not eat as much junk for stress relief." Not only that, but Theresa feels like she knows herself so much better now that she's in her 40s. She believes that she is where she's supposed to be.

Today's Latina business owners and leaders can help the next generation of women achieve greater economic, social, and political influence by being mentors.

# Chapter 7:
# Carolina Jovenich

CEO
Caroline Promotions, Inc.
*www.carolinepromotions.com*

## Valuable Learning Experiences

Ana Carolina Jovenich is a third-generation Argentinean who was born in Buenos Aires. Her mother's family is of German descent; her father's family is of Spanish descent. Carolina had a quiet, humble, and work-oriented upbringing in a middle-class family. Her mother, Mirta Schefer, was a rural schoolteacher. When she met Carolina's father, Santiago Jovenich, and they began to raise a family, Mirta decided to dedicate all of her time to her children and thus became a homemaker. Carolina's father was an entrepreneur. He first established a travel agency, and some years later, turned to real estate and started a company.

From her father, Carolina learned about responsibility. Although she was not interested in the real-estate industry, watching him conduct business was a valuable learning experience for her. He was always impeccably dressed; he wore a suit Monday through Sunday. That demonstrated to Carolina that he was a hard-worker who felt that the effort put forth in one's appearance was just as important as every other type of effort in the business world. Carolina feels proud that her father was a well-known, recognized, and respected man in the community.

Aside from his sharp sense of style, it probably helped that he was an imposing figure at over six-feet tall. She says, "He was like a walking monument; everyone knew him and welcomed him like he was a star." When Carolina was sixteen years old, he suffered a heart attack. After that he was forced to take a leave of absence from running his business due to his delicate state of health. That was a personally trying time for Carolina and her family. The responsibility of providing for the family then shifted to her mother. Given that her mother is an extremely talented woman, it was not surprising that she showed an enormous capacity for the business, taking the company to a new level with creative ideas and hard work. When Mirta took over the real estate-business, she conducted most of the work over the phone in order to look after Carolina's ill father.

Her mother is not afraid of anything. Carolina remembers how oftentimes, her mother would quickly switch roles, going from being well-dressed in greeting clients to getting down on her hands and knees to make repairs needed on the apartments they were renting. From these memories, Carolina learned that an entrepreneur's prominence is not diminished if she performs the work necessary to keep her business going, no matter how menial it may seem.

### Promotions

In 1989, Carolina worked for the first time on a promotional event as a hostess. Her older brother Santiago, who owns his own business, a branding agency in Argentina called Latin Brand Lovers, was the creative director of a famous clothing company and invited her to work on an event. Doing so, Carolina enjoyed herself. As a result, she then began working for different agencies that provided models and hostesses for product launches, sampling, and promotional events.

Eventually, Carolina tapped into her entrepreneurial spirit when at twenty-one, she started organizing small fashion shows and coordinating promotions at big concerts and trade shows. Her business in Argentina was beginning to blossom when she was presented with the opportunity to travel to Los Angeles.

## Excitement Turns to Trepidation

When she arrived in the U.S., Carolina's excitement turned to trepidation. Soon after, she realized that her lack of proficiency in the English language would cause her several awkward moments. Carolina's Argentinean Spanish was not interpreted the same as what she calls "neutral" Spanish. Carolina remembers many instances in which her Argentinean Spanish caused her to have misunderstandings with vendors.

As these language misunderstandings became more frequent, it reaffirmed what Carolina had been suspecting for some time. She needed to learn English as well as a more general "neutral Spanish" to be able to better interact with the many different nationalities that share the Spanish language in Southern California. Another occasion she remembers fondly was a time when she came up with a unique concept for advertising Spanish soap operas on the radio. Carolina invented a character that respectfully stereotyped a blue-collar housewife. The housewife was portrayed hand-washing clothes while talking to her friend about the latest developments in the soap opera. Carolina used to write the scripts for the radio spot promotion and so she had to write using a whole new vocabulary including Mexican and Central American idioms. This is where what she had learned about "neutral" Spanish came into play.

Carolina learned "neutral" Spanish by listening to the way friends from different countries spoke. However, since Carolina had yet to master this new skill when she started writing commercials for a Spanish-language channel, her best friend, Mexican-born Laura Rodriguez, "translated" her Argentinean Spanish into "neutral" Spanish.

## Fiesta Broadway

During her time at one of the Spanish television stations, Carolina volunteered to help with the distribution of premiums at Fiesta Broadway, the second-largest Hispanic event in the United States. The event attracts about 500,000 people in one day. The city shuts down Broadway Street in downtown Los Angeles, turning that strip into advertising galore. The biggest current talent is brought onto the two stages every year to perform, attracting thousands of spectators. In the meantime, advertisers have their different products or services sampled by hundreds of people at their booths. From this experience, Carolina quickly identified a need for her craft. Consequently, she decided to fill the void in promoting specifically to the Hispanic market and improve the quality of the execution with innovative ideas and better-trained bilingual brand ambassadors. She thus began the journey toward creating her own business. After that realization, she proceeded to obtain information on how to start a business. She was told to simply "get the 'Fictitious Business Name' application," pay about $6.00, and register the business. Carolina did all of that, and then opened a bank account. Run from a room in her apartment, Caroline Promotions was born on September 15, 1995.

Carolina was determined to make her business known. She began by creating business cards in a machine at the mall and then handing them to everyone with whom she was able to speak in Spanish. Promoting her staffing agency was a big priority. The agency consisted of bilingual staffers, unlike Carolina who was still struggling with English. To try to better her English, Carolina attended UCLA Extension and enrolled in a Practical English program. The program was a language-intensive experience where Carolina was in class eight hours a day for several weeks. She was forced to learn the language since the other students only spoke other foreign languages and only way they could communicate was by speaking English. It turned out that Carolina has a natural affinity for language acquisition.

## Mentors

It was also at Fiesta Broadway, that Carolina met Victor Meza, who not only became her mentor and good friend, but who also believed in her and her vision so much that he became her first client. Soon after meeting Carolina, Victor called upon her to staff an event for Mobile Oil Corporation at a trade show. After she executed the event, he asked her to submit an invoice. Since Carolina was still learning English, she had no idea what an invoice was. So Victor drew it on a napkin for her, and that's when she finally realized what he was talking about.

Carolina states, "I owe much of my success to both my friends and clients who most of the time end up being one and the same, as they keep supporting my determination to succeed." It was not until she began to take on more consecutive projects that she was able to quit her day jobs and dedicate all her time to her business.

## *Libélulas*

Some time after that came an extremely trying period in Carolina's life that ultimately led her to where she is today. She was on a business trip in 2002 when she realized her marriage was ending because her husband had been unfaithful. Carolina was only scheduled for four hours of free time during that trip so she decided to visit the Oklahoma City Memorial to try to clear her mind and alleviate her devastation. This allowed her to contemplate all of the negative things that had recently transpired. She was standing at the fountain looking at her reflection when suddenly, a mass of dragon-flies (*libélulas*) appeared all around her. When she looked at her reflection again, the dragonflies had filled the shape of her body in the shadow of the fountain. The dragonflies she knew from Argentina were not very beautiful but actually, rather scary.

Carolina was readying her camera when the dragonflies left as quickly as they had come, but not before making a lasting impression on her. She was in awe of the beautiful green-and-blue shade of the tiny animals. In the moment when the dragonflies were around her, Carolina felt a sense of calm that had eluded her for some time. All of the sadness she'd been experiencing dissipated, and at that instant she knew everything was going to be OK for her. When she returned home she still had to deal with a difficult divorce and many other arduous situations, but now, each time she sees a dragonfly, it feels like a breath of fresh air is injected into her lungs. They allowed her to breathe when she needed to breathe the most.

Later, Carolina found out that the meaning of 'dragonfly' in Japanese is "new light and happiness." One day, while shopping at an arts-and-crafts store, she came across a hole puncher that made dragonfly cutouts. Coincidentally, Carolina was in the process of changing her business card, so she decided to incorporate the dragonfly as the symbol and logo of her company, starting with her business card. Now, the symbol of the creatures that helped get her through a very difficult time has become a unique business card that helps people remember her.

## Limitations

While Carolina determined the creative direction her company would take, she worked on building a Web site for herself. She worked on the Web site on and off for two and one-half years. Once she was ready to make it public, she realized she didn't know how the programming process worked. Then she asked a friend if he knew anyone who could do it for her, and he volunteered to do it himself. It turned out that he was a professional in the information-technology field. He put a whole new Web site together in less than one week, and it included the placement of the dragonfly and the teal color, both representative of the company. It was then that Carolina realized she had spent too much time trying to do some-thing that was not her within her realm of expertise. Her advice to those considering starting a business is, "Find out your limitations and once you do, let experts take care of the things you can't do well. It will pay off for your business in the long run." The Web site her friend designed is still working well for Caroline Promotions, Inc., and as he is now the company's IT person, he keeps it updated.

Caroline Promotions Inc. helps companies develop new ways to market their products and services at marketing events through grass-roots promotional campaigns. The company provides high-quality event and field-marketing services as well as bilingual staffing for companies targeting Latino and general-market consumers throughout the U.S. Their creative marketing approach, which includes street teams, technology and mobile marketing, is designed to create brand awareness and generate incremental sales for clients showcasing products and services to consumers in different environments, such as concerts, sporting events, festivals and street fairs.

As CEO of Caroline Promotions, Carolina cofounded the first-ever bilingual bridal show, "Expo Novia Latina" in 2003, which helped bridge the gap between first- and third-generation Latinas when planning a wedding. Carolina and her partners organized an incredible event, incorporating Brazilian dancers, a Uruguayan group, and many other great attractions. It was a very well produced event. Carolina was proud of her team; she had never seen anything executed that well before. Now, there are many trade shows available in Spanish, but Expo Novia Latina was the first bilingual one.

## Formal Corporation

In 2002 Carolina went to work full time for her company, then in 2005, she decided to change her company's legal structure from sole proprietorship to a formal corporation, and she moved into an office building for the first time. The offices are located in the city of Glendale. In just over a decade, Caroline Promotions has grown into a well-known field-marketing agency with tremendous customer satisfaction that has led to an inescapable fact: Most of her clients have come from referrals. Her company has provided high-quality event/field-marketing services for several Fortune 500 companies while helping them develop innovative ways to market an array of products and services in the Hispanic market. Clients hire Caroline Promotions not only because of the great customer service and flawless execution, but also because it specializes in marketing to the Hispanic community. Carolina's clients can tell the company is special. They treat clients extremely well. She makes herself extremely accessible, not only to her clients but also to the people who work for her. Fortunately, Caroline Promotions is in demand, so much so that they are planning to expand in order to handle more accounts. To this end, Carolina has begun to hire and train more people.

Her thriving spirit has caused her to improve her management skills by enrolling in courses like the Pepperdine Business Certificate Program offered by the Latin Business Association (LBA) and the National Association of Women Business Owners' (NAWBO) PEAK Leadership Academy program taught by Yvonne Randle, coauthor of *Growing Pains: Transitioning from an Entrepreneurship to a Professionally Managed Firm.*

## Leading by Example

Carolina leads by example and with integrity. Following in the large footsteps of her parents, she has a genuine commitment to building a profitable business and succeeding at the highest level as an entrepreneur. She believes in continually embracing change, thinking outside the box, and remaining open to new opportunities. Self-sufficiency and enthusiasm are an integral part of her credo at Caroline Promotions. Her energy emanates from the satisfaction she gets from sharing her positive vision and providing a supportive hand to anyone who needs it. With an amazing capacity to inspire others, Jovenich takes pride in creating career-development opportunities for young Latinos; she hopes that this will be their stepping stone toward growing into further leadership roles.

She states, "My strength stems from the support I receive from my family, especially my mother and younger brother, Christian Jovenich. He has always been one of my biggest supporters." Christian has contributed to the growth of Caroline Promotions, and became Director of Operations. Using his great leadership and problem-solving skills, he has helped the company to execute flawlessly in many events and is helping Carolina to establish a branch in Las Vegas. Another source of pride for Carolina is the fact that she helps support her family; she is monetarily self-reliant and self-sufficient. She is thankful that she is able to express her passion for the work she enjoys doing. Because of her dream, Carolina has made it possible for others to work. Through her company's contributions, she is able to offer others the opportunity to work and grow; those things give her a well-deserved sense of accomplishment. Not surprisingly, although her company has not reached its full potential, Carolina has received two offers from other companies that wish to partner with Caroline Promotions, Inc.

## Creating Jobs

Carolina is grateful that her dream has helped create jobs for many young Latinos. As a business owner, she feels it is her duty to help others by offering and providing educational opportunities to the next generation of Latinos so that they can expand their knowledge and potential, thereby fostering an environment of growth, not only within the company, but also on a personal level. For many of the young staffers that her company employs, their first check from Caroline Promotions is the first check they receive in their lives, which represents their first step into the workforce.

Another idea Carolina promotes to people in search of their dreams is, "Don't be afraid to ask for help." When Carolina was first trying to start her business, she told anyone who would listen about her dreams and aspirations. After a while, the people to whom she had communicated her dreams responded by helping her to achieve them. Such examples include Oscar Luna, the friend who designed her Web site and Gerardo Prat, who has helped her on many occasions. Carolina says, "There was always someone who knew someone who knew how to do things." Another mantra Carolina has held on to over the years is, "Don't be afraid to hire someone who knows more than you in certain aspects of the business. You can't be an expert in everything." She has learned that through trial and error, but says it has been very valuable information for her business.

When it comes to innovations for the future of Caroline Promotions, Carolina says that for the first time, she needs to hire more executives. For a long time it was only her at the top level of the company. But now, her brother and the new team will make sure everything is done the Caroline Promotions, Inc., way—with great customer service and great attention to detail.

For her company, Carolina envisions a future where Caroline Promotions will grow to a point of managing itself as a well-oiled corporate machine. When that occurs, she will have time to further pursue other interests such as continuing to travel the world and exploring other cultures thereby promoting the empowerment of women and encouraging respect for minority cultures, especially Hispanics, in the United States.

In 2003 Carolina was featured alongside the Argentinean and Uruguayan Consuls In the Argentinean magazine *El Suplemento*—as one of the "Personalities of the Year," showcasing her as a shining example, leader, and entrepreneur within the Hispanic community. Carolina is a member of the Latin Business Association (LBA), National Association of Female Executives (NAFE), and National Association of Women Business Owners (NAWBO).

# Chapter 8:
# Martha Lugo-Aguayo

Vice President/Managing Partner
Spectrum Benefits Group

At the tender age of four, Martha Lugo-Aguayo's favorite thing to do in the world was tap dance. Imagine living in an apartment in New York with a young daughter who tapped around all day long! With this came the loud rap on the radiator from the downstairs neighbor telling Martha's mom that her daughter's tap dancing was not welcomed.

When she was six, Martha danced her way to *Your Show of Shows* with Sid Caesar and Imogene Coca. After the show, Martha was asked why she was not nervous when performing. To her mother's astonishment, her response was, "Why should I be nervous? I'm not so good." Martha's mother responded, "You are good. You are very good." It was then that Doña Violeta realized it was going to be very difficult for her daughter to recognize and accept her accomplishments in life. Praise and glory were not what Martha was looking for; Her happiness was in making sure everyone else around her was happy.

### Tireless Parents

Although she was a stay-at-home mom, Martha's mother was a lady who never tired. If her daughters were invited anywhere, the sewing machine would go on all night until that special dress was completed and ready for the occasion. The woman behind her husband's career, Doña Violeta was always in the background lending support and giving well-taken advice. Now at age eighty-five, with her short-term memory failing, she fights the memory battle everyday with strong determination.

Martha's father is a self-made man whose intelligence, positive outlook on life, and great sense of humor set the standard for her family. His motto is, "go for the stars; all you have to do is reach out and touch them." Another family motto that stayed with Martha throughout her life is, "You can be stripped of everything—home, car, and all the material possessions in the world—but you cannot be stripped of your knowledge, what is in your heart, or your deter-mination to succeed." Even without a formal education, her father retired from the post office as Chief Operations Officer for San Juan Puerto Rico and the Virgin Islands. Talk about an amazing example.

Martha's sister Nayda embarked on a successful banking career and motherhood. She cared for her only daughter who was afflicted with cerebral palsy and who later died at the age of twenty-one, but her vibrancy and determination did not wither. Nayda considers herself fortunate to have been able to care for a daughter who brought her only happiness. Although younger, Martha's sister has been her confidant and a great inspiration. She resides in Puerto Rico with her husband and two boys, enjoying the benefits of being a grandmother.

Soon after Martha's television appearance, her father accepted a transfer with the post office to San Juan, Puerto Rico, where he wanted to raise his two daughters. Raising his daughters near family where they could learn and live their culture and enjoy a good qual-ity of life was his ultimate goal. Life in Puerto Rico was wonderful for Martha and her family. The freedom of being able to ride a bicycle on the streets and enjoy summers with close relatives in the country was ideal. Both Martha and her sister went to Catholic school to continue their education in Puerto Rico.

## An Entrepreneur Is Born

Martha's first experience as a budding entrepreneur occurred while she worked at Fort Brooke, Army Headquarters in San Juan, Puerto Rico, in the Civilian Personnel Office. A close friend of the family was liquidating his antiquated inventory of silk stockings. When Martha asked if she could buy it, she should have been alerted by his puzzled look about the oddity of her offer. But she did not budge. After what seemed like thousands of trips later from his stock room to her house (she moved the inventory on her bike), Martha started her business. Each day she took a dozen boxes of silk stockings to work to sell to coworkers. She came home empty-handed, checked her inventory, and prepared her next dozen boxes to take to work the next day.

Martha must have been extremely persistent since she even sold stockings to the soldiers to send home to their relatives or girlfriends. Now, *this* took a lot of nerve! They could have bought them at the PX at a discount. Even more puzzling was the fact that pantyhose were the new rage, and Martha was selling silk stockings. It was a great surprise to all involved (including their dear friend who sold her his inventory) that she sold all the stockings, made a huge profit, and celebrated by taking her family to Saint Thomas for a mini vacation. Martha's father was convinced that she could sell, but preferred that she become a teacher or nurse and not take any risks.

## A Desire to See the World

Not convinced at the time that she wanted to pursue a career as a civil servant, she recalls, "When you're young, job security is not a priority." She had a desire to see the world, so she decided to change careers: a decision that was extremely upsetting to her family. Martha's next venture was to become an airline stewardess (now called a "flight attendant"). Coming from a conservative Puerto Rican Family, this career choice was short-lived for Martha due to family pressure. They were always reminding her that she attended college, but all she was doing was serving people in the sky. They thought it would be better if she stopped having fun and embarked upon a successful career. Finding a husband and getting married would also have been acceptable. The fact that she represented Airspur, the commuter airline she worked for in New York during an advertising campaign, and that free travel was available for the entire family was not an enticement to them. Her family would prefer to see her working in an office and establishing her future.

After her stint in the aviation business, Martha went to work for the Commonwealth Oil Refining Company, the company responsible for her transfer to New York City. Moving to New York City at the age of twenty-six was the adventure of a lifetime. A couple of other female employees her age were also transferred to the Big Apple. Her first adventure in the big city was transferring the many boxes of personal belongings that were sent to Commonwealth Oil Refining Company to her apartment. With no car and only the assistance of her roommate, they transferred the boxes on a blanket through Grand Central Station onto the train and then to their apartment. As Martha looks back on this misadventure, she views it as quite an embarrassment. She says, "New York is the city where you either make it or go back home. I was determined that, although I loved Puerto Rico and eventually wanted to return, I would not return until I was ready and had been successful."

However, New York was the place where she had her first encounter with people's ignorance. She was asked if she was a minority. Having never heard this term before, she thought they were asking if she was a Democrat or a Republican. So her answer was, "I never talk politics and I never discuss party affiliations." The look on the face of the person inquiring was priceless! Then, Martha was shocked to find out that she was indeed, a minority.

## Getting to *Sesame Street*

After two years of living in New York, a close friend set up an appointment for Martha to interview with the highly acclaimed producers of *Sesame Street*—now known as Children's Television Workshop. Not knowing what *Sesame Street* was, Martha interviewed and mistakenly shared this information with her very young nephews. Without having the job or even thinking about accepting the job, her nephews had spread the word through the entire Long Island neighborhood where they lived, that their "Titi Cookie" was working at *Sesame Street* and that she knew Big Bird. Martha then suffered sleepless nights and prayed that the job would be offered to her. When the job was offered, she didn't think twice. Needless to say, she was a very popular aunt.

At Children's Television Workshop, Martha held various positions. It was there that she blossomed professionally. Martha had numerous mentors and she particularly admired the founder Joan Ganz Cooney. Her parents gave her the wisdom that formed her morally and emotionally and which guided her intellectually. Their pillar of strength gave her character, their trust in her gave her confidence, and their love gave her security. She states, "They are definitely my foundation."

## A Son Is Born

Professionally, Martha's friend and supervisor at Children's Television Workshop, Sue Cushman, gave her the confidence she lacked for believing that she could be successful as a professional career woman. Sue's determination to be successful rubbed off on

Martha. She admired Sue's honesty in dealing with everyday challenges in the business world. As Vice President of Administration and Chief Financial Officer for Children's Television Workshop in the '70s, Sue was a woman in her thirties doing a job usually held by men. She placed her confidence in Martha and promoted her to Director of Human Resources. Sue was there when Martha needed support, but mostly she left Martha on her own to grow into a position that had been held by men at that time; Martha was only twenty-six years old.

After Martha married in July of 1976, she left Children's Television Workshop and moved to Washington, D.C. In leaving Children's Television Workshop, Martha also left behind a support group of individuals who had nurtured her professionally and a company that had given her the opportunity to gain invaluable practical experience, which in turn allowed her to become a confident businesswoman. Washington, D.C., was a world of its own. After she married, Martha decided to hyphenate her name, but this practice came to an end in Washington, D.C. When she and her husband wanted to buy a home, she found that the hyphenation was not acceptable.

Washington, D.C. is where Martha's son David was born. Because Martha lived in a place where she did not have family or a support system, she decided to become a stay-at-home mom. Martha states, "I have never regretted the time I took to enjoy my son as a baby. I would make the same decision again today." In 1983, when David turned three years old, Martha and her family moved to England, where her husband had taken a job.

According to Martha, "My European experience was what I call icing on the cake." They traveled throughout Europe and absorbed customs like a sponge. Much was learned throughout Martha's European experiences; however, two especially important lessons learned were how to manage her time, and improvisational decision-making, all with a four-year-old in tow. Both of these newly acquired skills were necessary in her bourgeoning entrepreneurial career.

Martha took a detour when returning to the United States by spending a year with her son in Puerto Rico in 1990. That gave David the opportunity that Martha's parents had given her. David spent time with loving relatives, learned his culture—which he absorbed immediately—and learned to read and write Spanish. This was a gift for him to embrace for life. Returning to the United States was not easy. Martha's family had changed and assimilated to customs, many of which they were not aware. David had an English accent and they craved different foods. They missed the change of seasons, touring museums, and the easy accessibility of vacationing in other European cities.

### Flowers by Martha

Martha soon decided she needed to put some of the skills she had learned in Puerto Rico to good use. While there, she had taken a floral-design course and decided that this would be a great way to embark on a business venture. This is how Flowers by Martha started in 1991. Martha says, it was "great fun being creative, enjoying nature and the bounties of beautiful flowers. The shortcoming was that the hours were horrible." Unfortunately, the holidays were focused on business, not family. The busiest times of the year for florists are Valentines' Day, Mother's Day, Thanksgiving, and Christmas. The floral shop was a nightmare. No financial planning went into it at all. It was something Martha did to satisfy her artistic side, although she doesn't complain because she was surrounded by beautiful flowers! Most of the shopping for supplies went onto a credit card. Martha did a very wise thing, as the money came in the door, the credit-card bill was paid. So the payments were made on a monthly basis from the profits until the credit card was paid in full.

Though the business was home-based, it grew to be extremely successful. Martha even designed flowers for Gladys Knight. However, the success of Flowers by Martha was short-lived. With the floral industry moving into the supermarkets and wholesalers selling to the public, the handwriting of the business was on the wall. So it was back to the drawing board three years after she started her own business! That experience taught her how to work under pressure, deal with clients, meet deadlines, and how devastating it is to be in competition with giants.

## A Life-Changing Experience

Like most successful women, it took a life-changing experience to move from being an employee and dreamer to a person who turned her dreams into reality. Life moves rapidly and provides unbelievable surprises; sorting through these either makes you or breaks you. Martha's life change came after twenty-five years of marriage. Divorce is not easy; it takes its toll. With many nerve-racking decisions to make and very little time or space for trial and error in her business ventures, Martha knew that survival was the name of the game. At the age of fifty-three, when most of her associates were planning on exiting their careers, Martha was taking on the responsibility of becoming a partner in a business.

Martha is not a person who tolerates failure. The stifling haze that resulted from both a failed marriage and floral-business venture was not a long-term option for Martha. She took a long look at the past to determine on which capabilities she could capitalize to make the partnership work. Martha's motto is, "The past gives us the tools to use in the present; the present gives us the tools to dream and work to fulfill our future. Do not dwell in the past. It is a tool and not a state. Live and enjoy the present, and the future will come naturally." Martha undertook a search for her strengths, weaknesses, and the lessons that could be garnered from her previous mistakes.

Martha spent seven years raising her son in England where the only common dominator between her and everyone else was the language. Through this experience, Martha learned survival skills and how to function in a society that was very different from that of Puerto Rico. Through retrospection, Martha was able to capitalize on past experiences and employment history in order to move forward in searching for a new career. After twelve years at Children's Television Workshop as Director of Human Resources, Martha had gained corporate-world experience and a multitude of people skills, including the ability to work with a diverse group of nationalities and to be culturally sensitive.

## Spectrum Benefits Group

The career she chose was at Spectrum Benefits Group. There, she found a very nice work environment and extremely convenient location. The offices were located across the street from her son's school where Martha spent a lot of time volunteering or chauffeuring kids to and from games. Being a mom and raising David was her number-one priority. David moved on to a great high school, Loyola High School, an all boy Jesuit College Preparatory high school in Los Angeles. This was quite a sacrifice since driving to and from school was a day-long event (the drive from the city of Woodland Hills to Los Angeles is very long!). David graduated from Northwestern University in 2003 with three majors! Martha could not have been more proud.

Unlike other entrepreneurs, Martha became a partner in an existing business with a great reputation. The challenge was taking this business to the next level. At Spectrum Benefits Group, a full-service broker in California and other states, she designs employee benefits and insurance services for companies of all sizes. Separating themselves from companies that provided similar services was their goal.

With David all grown up and spending time in sports and socializing with friends, it was time for Martha to expand her horizons. The empty-nest syndrome was something she wanted to avoid. As an advocate of "being involved" and a firm believer in always using your brains to full capacity, she felt that finding a position close to home and to David would enable her to do both. Martha decided to embark upon a new career to boost her self-esteem and also to show David that women are capable of many things, including being mothers, wives, and career-women. In the back of her mind was also the fact that she needed to prepare herself to be independent again.

With Spectrum Benefits, no real planning went into Martha's decision to become a partner in this existing business. Later, someone told her that women interested in the business world come with a "we'll make it work" sensibility. The sale of a home and all of her savings went into this venture, and it was well worth it.

## Changes

Martha's first change at Spectrum Benefits in 1997 was to have a fully bilingual and culturally sensitive staff (English/Spanish) to provide their clients and their client's employees with service in their preferred language. The next change to be made was to become creative in designing benefits that would suit the budget and needs of their clients and those of their employees. For Spectrum Benefits Group, it is not about selling a product but listening to their clients, learning about their company, and then researching to see which employee benefits will work for them.

With the changing market, they also have to be both informed of new trends in the industry and knowledgeable about government regulations affecting their clients. Spectrum Benefits' goal is to do business in today's market without jeopardizing the *service* to their clients. They have moved to a level of high name recognition with an outstanding reputation, but they will not stop there.

Growth is continual; they still meet with consultants to assess how to move to the next level. Training is an integral part of their agenda. Memberships in various organizations and associations give them the opportunity to learn from other business and to contribute sharing their expertise as well. Martha is a firm believer that networking works. Many years ago, she started by gathering together five friends. The purpose of the meeting was to get to know one another, and for the group to continue to have gatherings by inviting one person from the gathering and adding new people at the same time. That became a powerful group of women. They could refer to one another for almost anything.

Being a Latina can be both beneficial and disadvantageous in her industry. Martha says, "Many times when meeting with a prospect, I can judge whether being a woman, or even more so a 'Hispanic woman,' has either helped or hindered bringing the prospect on as a client." She has heard everything from "You are from Puerto Rico?" followed by, "I loved Westside Story!" to "You don't look Puerto Rican." Says Martha, "Thank God for thick skin and knowing that tolerance is a virtue."

## Advice

As far as advice goes, Martha notes that the world is getting smaller and positive changes toward our gender and ethnicity will continue to take place. She encourages women to be involved, not to shy away from their culture or language and to be proud of who they are. It has taken a multitude of women to pave the way, and according to her, "We need you to continue educating, becoming entrepreneurs and to stand tall for future generations." Martha believes we owe it to future generations of Latinas and Hispanic women to share our stories of adversity, the lessons of life and how these have affected us; by doing this, one may touch the life of a young Latina woman looking for direction or a role model. To that end, giving back to the community is also a priority for Martha. The future of her businesses and our country rests in our children's hands. Charities that deal with the advancement of our children's future are the ones with which she has chosen to be affiliated including Childhelp USA. and Padres Contra el Cancer. Today, so much information is available from lenders and non-profit organizations. One that comes to mind is CHARO. They have incubator programs and have guest speakers to bring the information to the young entrepreneur. The SBA also does a wonderful job promoting how they can assist.

Most of Martha's public speaking is about Spectrum Benefits Group, regarding what they do and how they are different from other brokers. Consequently, it is a very comfortable subject for her. It was not until recently that Martha has begun to speak about herself. She says, "I'd rather focus on the business than my personal life. The only exception is if my experiences would make a difference in another person's life." She also states, "Sharing what you do for a living is not boasting. I call it advertising without a charge!"

In order to survive the challenges Martha has endured, she's had to take each day as a stepping stone to a better, richer life. So, when honors are bestowed upon her, she finds them difficult to accept because she says, "Life alone has honored me with blessings. The future looks good with a wonderful son embarked upon a beautiful career and with a partner who shares my life and goals. So it's never too late to begin as an entrepreneur!"

### Anchors

When people ask Martha, "Insurance is boring. Do you have any interpersonal emotional moments?" her response is, "I guess it is not Hollywood, but to me it is a challenge." Her company meets people every day and tries to assist them with their needs. Today, society is dealing with the uninsured as a problem and they are trying to assist by making companies aware that they can integrate social benefits with the benefits they currently offer their employees. Most companies offer benefits for the employee only, (whether paying for full coverage or cost sharing) very rarely do they cost share in benefits for dependents. We educate the employer and employees on social benefits available, for example,

Healthy Families, Medicare, and other resources. This advice is given without Spectrum Benefits gaining monetary compensation.

## Measurement of Success

According to Martha, success is measured in many forms and, in our world, monetary compensation is a primary focus—it would an empty existence if this were the only measurement for success. So when asked about her personal metric for success, her answer is, "Success is when life feels good, your state of mind is good, and you are doing what makes you happy."

Martha's advice is, "go slow and research, research, research your business idea. Talk about it among trusted business advisors and mentors. Listen and study their advice. Have a business plan, have capital and have a fall back position. The first few years of any venture are risky and even after the first few years, keeping the business fresh, innovative and achieving financial stability is a challenge. Continue learning your business. Knowledge is a tool and keeping abreast of new trends is a must. Join networking organizations and affiliations to help grow your business. Know your market and listen to it and make timely changes if needed."

## Thriving

Spectrum Benefits will continue to thrive, and as far as Martha is concerned, retirement is a word she has difficulty saying aloud. Her ultimate goal is to continue to grow and to be part of Spectrum Benefits as an owner in an advisory-consultant capacity.

At this point in time, Martha does not have an exit strategy. Taking Spectrum Benefits Group to another level is taking most of her and her partner's time and all their energy. Very soon they hope to announce areas in which they will be expanding to include Financial Planning for the young professionals and for the mature adults who are ready to plan retirement. Unfortunately, full details of the expansion cannot be released in time for the printing of this chapter. Many legal ramifications and other negotiations are still on the table. The anticipation of new projects keeps Martha going and according to her, that is what keeps her "young, energized, and open-minded."

## Muchas Gracias

Many times when conducting enrollment meetings, Martha will give her cell-phone number to clients and their employees. She has been warned many times not to do this because it will be abused, and she may never get a good night's rest. To these warnings, she replies, "If abuse comes in the form of assisting Juanito when his wife was in labor and her ID card was off by one number and the hospital could not find her in the system, then so be it." Gratification came Monday morning when the call announcing, "It's a boy!" followed by, *"Muchas gracias!"* was on the answering machine. That's the kind of woman she is: a hard worker with a wonderful heart ready and willing to help the world in the profession she has chosen for herself.

# Section II:
# Establishing Your Business as a Latina

# Chapter 9:
# Establishing Your Business as a Latina

The remarkable stories of these women have inspired me and provided knowledge that has helped me to grow personally and in my business. Even after thirty-five years as an entrepreneur, I have never stopped learning. I learned that none of the women began their journeys fully understanding what they were getting into. They all earned success by using common sense, taking risks, and ultimately, overcoming tremendous odds. There were cultural barriers, personal struggles, and remarkable sacrifices of every kind. The majority of the women had to struggle at it alone; few are fortunate enough to enjoy the support of an understanding husband. Those who have a life partner have taken advantage of it by sharing their business as well as their lives together. In the end, our families are the backbone of our lives, the unconditional supporters that have allowed us to thrive. Those who don't have this kind of support have to learn to make the best of their independence.

There were many common threads in the stories of these women. They provided numerous lessons. There are multiple opportunities to learn from the processes they went through to start their own businesses. The following is a reminder of some of the strengths and characteristics these Latina business owners posses, the reasons they have been successful, and the reasons you will be successful too:

## Necessary Strengths and Characteristics

- Vision
- Curiosity
- Passion
- Self-Confidence
- Focus
- Creativity
- Determination
- Intuition
- Desire
- Leadership
- Innovation
- Devotion to family values

- An adventurous spirit
- A belief in themselves
- The ability to overcome obstacles
- The need to do what they love
- The ability to handle success
- A desire for economic independence
- A desire to share knowledge
- Having and pursuing a dream
- The ability to accept advice
- High tolerance for risk

And after reading the personal as well as professional stories of these thriving entrepreneurs, you must be encouraged and motivated to start or continue your own business. Whether it's a service or a product you have in mind, I would like to share with you some of the most fundamental principles you should understand before embarking on the journey to start your own business.

## Entrepreneurship Defined by a Latina

"An entrepreneur is an individual who undertakes to supply a good or service to the market for profit. Entrepreneurs will usually invest their own capital in a business and take on the risks associated with the investment."[14] Entrepreneurs create new products, build new industries, and bring new life to old industries. "By one count, entrepreneurs are the force behind two-thirds of the inventions and 95 percent of innovations made since WWII. Entrepreneurs play a significant role in the economy by creating major innovations, increasing the number of jobs, and providing opportunities for women, men, and minorities."[15]

Entrepreneurs must recognize that there is no one style of leadership that is effective and that there are significant differences in leadership style among organizations. I became a leader in my company as I started understanding my job more and more. Leadership is the process of influencing the members of the organization to build the various key aspects of the pyramid, creating a goal-congruent situation in which employees can satisfy their own needs by seeking to achieve the goals of the organization. Leadership is behavior oriented and goal-directed. The changing market has altered my vision at one time or another. Being a Latina has been an advantage and a disadvantage for me, if you remember my story.

**How to become an entrepreneur:** The ideal beginning is by completing academic programs in colleges and universities. For the past two decades, there has been tremendous growth in the number of majors and other educational opportunities for people seeking to become entrepreneurs. Another way to become an entrepreneur is by gaining practical experience by working part-time, full-time, or interning for business employers. Reading newspapers, magazine articles, and biographies of successful entrepreneurs will also prove beneficial, allowing you to learn how entrepreneurs handle the challenges of starting their businesses. Some of these publications that are especially helpful for Latinas include, *Entrepreneur Magazine, Latina Style Magazine,*

---

[14] Oxford Dictionary of Business
[15] Boone, Louis E., David L. and Kurtz. 2006. *Contemporary Business, 2006: Custom Version for Santa Monica College.* 11th ed. Mason: Thomson South-Western. P. 206.

*Hispanic Business Magazine, Hispanics, Inc., Latin Business, Fortune, Forbes,* and so on.

Owning a business is the dream of many Americans. Your dreams can only be achieved with the careful planning of which I am sure you are capable. As a Latina entrepreneur, you will need a plan to avoid pitfalls, to achieve your goals, and to build a profitable business.

## Is Entrepreneurship for You?

This is the most important question you can ask yourself, because nothing is guaranteed in business. There is no way to eliminate all the risks that come with starting a business. However, with a good plan in hand, preparation, and some insight, you can overcome such risks.

## Latinas' Strengths and Weaknesses

Start by evaluating your strengths and weaknesses as a potential owner of a small business. Carefully consider each one of the following questions:

- Are you a self-starter? It will be entirely up to you to develop projects, organize your time, and follow through on details.

- Are you self-motivated? No one will be behind you. The passion and initiative to get things done have to come from you.

- Do you deal well with different personalities? Business owners need to develop working relationships with many different people.

- How good are you at making decisions? Small-business owners are required to make decisions constantly—often quickly, independently, and under pressure.

- Do you have the physical and emotional stamina to run a business? Business ownership can be exciting, but it is also a lot of work. Can you face six or seven 12-hour workdays every week?

- How well do you plan and organize? Good organization of finances, inventory, schedules, and production can help you avoid many pitfalls. Is your drive strong enough? Running a business can be emotionally abrasive. Strong motivation will help you survive slowdowns and periods of burnout.

- How will the business affect your family? The first few years of business start-up can be hard on family life. It's important for family members to know what to expect, and for you to be able to trust that they will support you during this time. There may also be financial difficulties until the business becomes profitable, which could take months or years. You may have to adjust to a lower standard of living or put family assets at risk as collateral.

## Challenges of Latina Entrepreneurship

Success in business is never automatic. A business is like someone's life; it has ups and downs, and even sick days. It is not strictly based on luck—although a little never hurts. It depends primarily on the owner's foresight and organization. Even then, there are no guarantees. A small business may find itself especially vulnerable during an economic downturn, since it may have accumulated fewer resources than its large competitors to cushion a sales decline. Starting a small business is always risky, and the chance of success is slim. According to the U.S. Small Business Administration, roughly 50 percent of small businesses fail within the first five years. However, also keep in mind that Latinos are opening businesses in record numbers. *You* can become one of those numbers!

The primary disadvantages facing small businesses include:

- Lack of focus

- Inadequate financing

- Wrong location

- Over-investment in inventory or fixed assets

- Poor credit arrangements

- Use of business funds for personal reasons

- Unplanned growth

- Government regulations

- Not understanding your financial statements

- Inadequate management

- Not enough sales

- Inconsistency with quality of product or service

- Not having the right price

- Not understanding your competitors

- Not enough experience

- Lack of patience

- An unwillingness to work hard

These disadvantages aren't meant to scare you, but to prepare you for the difficult road ahead. They are not exclusive to the beginning of a business; instead, they continue to be obstacles throughout the duration of a business. Even after thirty-five years of being an entrepreneur, I am still struggling with many of these issues. However, with experience comes the ability to overcome these obstacles.

## My Greatest Business Satisfactions

There are many reasons to start your own business. For the right person, the advantages of business ownership far outweigh the risks. The following ten reasons have been my greatest business satisfactions:

1. Be your own boss and have independence.

2. It is honorable to create a business from scratch.

3. The hard work and long hours directly benefit you.

4. The growth potential is far greater.

5. A new venture is as exciting as it is risky.

6. There are endless challenges and opportunities for learning.

7. You make your own hours.

8. You can do what you want, when you want, and how you want.

9. You can improve your standard of living.

10. You will have financial and job security.

## Finding Your Niche

In choosing an idea for your business, the two most important considerations are 1) finding something you love to do and are good at doing, and 2) determining whether your idea can satisfy a need in the marketplace. When people willingly work hard doing something they love, the experience will likely bring personal fulfillment. Doing what makes you happy and being honest with yourself are the best guidelines for deciding on a business idea.

A market in its entirety is too broad in scope for any but the largest companies to tackle successfully. The best strategy for a small business is to divide demand into manageable market niches. Small operations can then offer specialized goods and services attractive to a specific group of prospective buyers.

There are undoubtedly some particular products or services you are especially suited to provide. Survey the market carefully and you will find opportunities. As an example, surgical instruments used to be sold in bulk to both small medical practices and large hospitals. One firm realized that the smaller practices could not afford to sterilize instruments after each use like hospitals did, so they were forced to simply dispose of them. The firm's sales representatives talked to surgeons and hospital workers to learn what would be more suitable for them. Based on this information, the company developed disposable instruments that could be sold in larger quantities at a lower cost. Another firm capitalized on the fact that hospital operating rooms must carefully count the instruments used before and after surgery. This firm met that particular need by packaging their instruments in pre-counted, customized sets for different forms of surgery.[16]

While researching your own company's niche, consider the results of your market survey. Analyzing the market will yield two things. First, you should have found the areas in which your competitors are already firmly situated. Second, by putting this information into a table or a graph, you can locate potential openings for your product or service. Try to find the right configuration of products, services, quality and price that will ensure the least direct competition. Unfortunately, there is no universally effective way to make these comparisons. Not only will the desired attributes vary from industry to industry, but there is also an imaginative element that cannot be formalized. For example, only someone who had already thought of developing prepackaged surgical instruments could use a survey to determine whether or not a market actually existed for them.

If you do target a new niche market, make sure that this niche does not conflict with your overall business plan. For example, a small bakery that makes cookies by hand cannot go after a market for inexpensive, mass-produced cookies, regardless of the demand.

## Basic Questions for Finding Your Niche

I also asked myself the following basic questions in addition to the previous list before starting Lulu's Dessert twenty-five years ago, and you should ask them of yourself before starting your own business.

1. Do you know who your customers will be?

2. Do you understand their needs and desires?

---

[16] Information for preceding paragraphs from www.sba.gov

3. Do you know where your customers live?

4. Will you be offering the kind of products or services they will buy?

5. Will your prices be competitive in quality and value?

6. Do you need a market analysis?

7. Do you understand how your business compares with your competitors?

8. Will your business be conveniently located for the people you plan to serve?

## Additional Aid for Finding Your Niche

1. List your interests and abilities. Include your values and beliefs, your goals and dreams, things you like and dislike doing, and your job experiences. The product or service you want to provide has to be something about which you feel motivated and passionate. Once you have done that, identify and briefly describe the business you plan to start.

2. Identify the product or service you plan to sell. Decide on a business that matches what you want and offers profit potential.

3. Make sure your product or service satisfies an unfilled need. Carefully evaluate existing goods and services, looking for ways you can improve them.

4. Make sure your product or service serves an existing market in which demand exceeds supply. Read newspapers and business and consumer magazines to learn about demographic and economic trends that identify future needs for products that no one yet offers.

5. Make sure your product or service is competitive based on its quality, selection, price, or location. Conduct marketing research

to determine whether your business idea will attract enough customers to earn a profit.

6. Learn as much as you can about the industry in which your new venture will operate, your merchandise or service, and your competitors. Read surveys that project growth in various industries.

If you recall, I had recently arrived in the U.S. with my Travel and Conventions Company already established when my life took an unexpected turn and I had to reinvent myself. I had to find a new business in order to stay in the U.S. since the only way I could work was for my own company. I was on the lookout for a new idea. As a consumer, I was looking for the traditional gelatin dessert from Mexico. That is when I decided to start a completely different business than the one that had originally brought me to the U.S. My niche was found and Lulu's Dessert became a reality.

## Planning Your Start-up

So far this checklist has helped you identify questions and problems you will face converting your idea into reality and determining if your idea is feasible. Through the evaluation of your strengths and weaknesses you have learned about your personal qualifications and deficiencies. Through your answers to the list for finding a niche, you have learned if there is a demand for your product or service.

The following is designed to help you plan your business start-up.

## Name and Legal Structure

You need to choose a name for your business. Then you have to choose whether to operate as a sole proprietorship, partnership, or corporation.

## Major Forms of Private Ownership

| Form of Ownership | Sole Proprietorship | Partnership | Corporation |
|---|---|---|---|
| Number of Owners | One Owner | Two or More Owners | Unlimited Number of shareholders; up to 75 shareholders for S corporations |
| Liability | Unlimited personal liability for business debt | Personal assests of any operating partner at risk from business creditors | Limited |
| Advantages | 1. Owner retains all profits 2. Easy to form and dissolve 3. Owner has flexibility | 1. Easy to form and dissolve 2. Can benefit from complementary management skills 3. Expanded financial capacity | 1. Limited financial liability 2. Specialized management skills 3. Expanded financial capacity 4. Economies of large-scale operations |
| Disadvantages | 1. Unlimited financial liability 2. Financial limitations 3. Management defeciencies 4. Lack of continuity | 1. Unlimited financial liability 2. Interpersonal conflicts 3. Lack of continuity 4. Difficult to dissolve | 1. Difficult and costly to form and dissolve 2. Tax disadvantages 3. Legal restrictions |

## Your Business and the Law

A person in business is not expected to be a lawyer but each business owner should have a basic knowledge of laws affecting the business. Here are some of the legal matters you should be acquainted with:

1. Know which licenses and permits you may need to operate your business. For this, you can call or visit your local city hall.

2. Know and understand the business laws you will have to obey.

3. Have a lawyer and an accountant who can advise you and help you with legal documents. One free resource you can take advantage of is the Small Business Administration's Small Business Development Centers.

4. The following are some examples of the things you should be aware of:

- Occupational Safety and Health Administration (OSHA) requirements

- Regulations covering hazardous material

- Local ordinances

- Federal Tax Code provisions pertaining to small business

- Federal regulations on withholding taxes and Social Security

- State Worker's Compensation laws

## Protecting Your Business

It is becoming increasingly important that attention be given to legal, security, and insurance protection for your business.

An entrepreneur will need to protect the rights to the name of the company, logos, packaging, trademarks, and inventions. Visit the U.S. Patent and Trademark Office at www.uspto.gov. There, you will find information on these processes along with forms to apply for a patent. Since 2000, inventors have been able to apply for patents online at this Web site.

There are several areas that should be covered. Have you examined the following categories of risk protection? Fire, Theft, Robbery, Vandalism, Accident and Product liability, and Worker's Compensation, among others.

## Business Records

- Be prepared to maintain complete records of sales income and expenses, accounts payable, and receivables.

- Determine how to handle payroll records, tax reports, and payments.

- Know what financial reports should be prepared and how to prepare them.

## What is a Business Plan and Why Do I Need One?

A business plan is a written document that articulates what a company's objectives are, how these objectives will be achieved, how the business will be financed, and how much money the company expects to generate. It precisely defines your business, identifies your goals, and serves as your firm's résumé. Its basic components include a current and pro forma balance sheet, an income statement, and a cash-flow analysis. It helps you allocate resources properly, handle unforeseen complications, handle daily challenges, and make the right decisions. As it provides specific and organized information about your company and how you will repay borrowed money, a good business plan is a crucial part of any loan package. Additionally, it can tell your sales personnel, suppliers, and others about your operations and goals. Some people mistakenly believe they only need a business plan if they are pursuing a venture capitalist or asking for a loan, but that is not the case; every small-business owner needs a business plan. The business plan is a living document that you will modify as you gain knowledge and experience. Many business owners share their business plans with their employees to foster a broader understanding of where the business is going.

## Why Do I Need to Define My Business in Detail?

It may seem silly to ask yourself, "What business am I really in?" but some owner/managers have gone broke because they never answered that question. One watch-store owner realized that most of his time was spent repairing watches, while most of his money was spent selling them. He finally decided he was in the repair business and discontinued the sales operations. His profits improved dramatically.

The importance of a comprehensive, thoughtful business plan cannot be overemphasized. Much hinges on it: outside funding, credit from suppliers, management of your operation and finances, promotion and marketing of your business, and achievement of your goals and objectives.

Despite the critical importance of a business plan, many entrepreneurs drag their feet when it comes to preparing a written document. They argue that the marketplace changes too fast for a business plan to be useful or that they just don't have enough time; but just as a builder won't begin construction without a blueprint, eager business owners shouldn't rush into new ventures without a plan.[17]

Before you begin writing your business plan, consider four core questions:

1. What service or product does your business provide and what needs does it fill?

2. Who are the potential customers for your product or service and why will they purchase it from you?

3. How will you reach your potential customers?

4. Where will you get the financial resources to start your business?

## How Do I Develop a Business Plan?

A business plan is a clear statement of a business identity. The plan should realistically assess the risks and obstacles specific to the business and present solutions for overcoming them. The following are items you should have on hand:

1. The company's name, history, mission statement, Strengths, Weaknesses, Opportunities, and Threats (SWOT) analysis, legal

---

[17] www.sba.gov

form of organization, location, financial highlights, owners or shareholders, and an executive-summary section including scope of work, methodology, summary of findings and recommendations, and human resources

2. Organization charts, list of key managers, consultants or directors, employee agreements

3. Marketing research, customer service, and information about the company's competitive analysis, strategic alternatives, and company goals, objectives, and strategies

4. Product information, including key goods and services, brochures, patents, licenses and trademarks, research, and development plans

5. Marketing plans and materials

6. Financial statements and forecasts

The length of the plan depends on the complexity of the company, whether the company is a start-up and what the plan will be used for. Regardless of size, the documents should be well-organized and easy to use, especially if the business plan is intended for external uses, such as to secure financing. Number all of the pages, include a table of contents, make sure the format is attractive and professional, include two or three illustrative charts or graphs, and highlight the sections and important points with headlines and bulleted lists.

## Tax ID Number

For a Federal Tax ID number, please contact the Internal Revenue Service for Form SS4. This form is available through their Web site at: http://www.irs.gov/pub/irs-pdf/fss4.pdf. You may call the IRS at 1-800-829-1040 and ask for the Small-Business Tax Kit #454.

Tax information for starting a business can be found by going to http://www.irs.gov/businesses/index.html. You will need to contact the Department of Revenue for state taxes, if there are any. You should consult your local telephone directory in the "State Government" section for the office in your state.

## Strategic Planning

Too many people think strategic planning is something meant only for big businesses, but it is equally applicable to small businesses. Strategic planning is matching the strengths of your business to available opportunities. To do this effectively, you need to collect, screen, and analyze information about the business environment. You also need to have a clear understanding of your business—its strengths and weaknesses—and develop a clear mission, goals, and objectives. Acquiring this understanding often involves more work than expected. You must realistically assess the business you are convinced you know well. In addition, strategic planning has become more important to business owners because technology and competition have made the business environment less stable and less predictable.

## Mission Statement

"The Mission Statement is a written explanation of an organization's business intentions and aims. It is an enduring statement of a firm's purpose, possibly highlighting the scope of operations, the market it seeks to serve and the ways it will attempt to set itself apart from competitors."[18] A mission statement provides direction for the company, customers, and the stakeholders. It answers the question, "What business are we really in?" for the employees, suppliers, and general public. It serves as the focus for all involved. Developing a mission statement is no easy feat, as it needs to be developed with the participation of key personnel in the company. This will ensure that the direction outlined accurately portrays the core purpose and capabilities of the organization. For example, following you will find:

---

[18] Boone, Louis E., David L. and Kurtz. 2006. *Contemporary Business, 2006: Custom Version for Santa Monica College.* 11th ed. Mason: Thomson South-Western. P. 273.

## Lulu's Desserts' Mission Statement:

Our Mission is to provide a variety of top-quality and healthy ready-to-eat desserts and snacks to satisfy the consumer's craving for flavorful products through continuous innovation. Lulu's Desserts' Mission includes the following components: to be profitable, to be the category leader, and to be both a national and international brand.

## Strengths, Weaknesses, Opportunities, and Threats

After creating a mission statement, a company needs an environmental analysis, also known as a SWOT assessment because it examines strengths, weaknesses, opportunities, and threats related to the company. The internal analysis evaluates the strengths and weaknesses of the company: what it does well and what it could improve. The external analysis evaluates the opportunities and threats, which are outside the control of the company.

| SWOT Summary | |
|---|---|
| **Internal Strengths** | **Internal Weaknesses** |
| Owner has over 25 years of experience in the dessert business with knowledge of Hispanic culture and culinary patterns | High concentration of sales in a few accounts |
| **External Opportunities** | **External Threats** |
| Rapidly growing Hispanic population in traditionally under-served neighborhoods | Potential increases in raw material costs |

## Goals, Objectives, and Strategies

Goals are broad business results that a business is committed to achieving. Objectives are quantifiable targets. They are more concrete statements than a mission statement. In today's business environment, more businesses are setting clear objectives for performance standards other than profitability. Strategies are the actions that will be taken to accomplish the stated objectives.

## Corporate Goals, Objectives, and Strategies

| Functional Area | Goals | Objectives | Strategies |
|---|---|---|---|
| Marketing | Increase Revenue | Increase Total Revenue | Develop New Products |
| Operations | Reduce Products Costs | Decrease Unit Product Cost by 10% Over Three Years | Optimize inventory stocks |
| Human Resources | Develop & Maintain a Supportive Organization Structure | Remain Adaptable & Flexible | Develop and Update Documentation |
| Accounting | Develop Accurate Product Cost Information | Comply with GAAP | Allocate Direct Labor Costs to Individual Product Lines |
| Finance | Improve Profitability, Activity, Liquidity, and Leverage | Prepare Monthly Cash Flow Statement | Analyze Monthly Income Statement and Set New Reasonable Objectives |

## Human Resources

Human Resources represents another critical input in every economic system. Human Resources includes anyone who works, from a CEO to a self-employed auto mechanic. This category encompasses both the physical labor and the intellectual input contributed by workers.

Since a company's success depends largely on the commitment and talents of its people, a growing number of firms are measuring and rewarding managers' performance in retaining employees in attracting qualified job candidates. Similarly, many companies consider workforce diversity to be a source of competitive advantage in serving various customer groups and thinking creatively.

The business owner must also plan how to attract and keep good employees with the right combination of pay, benefits, and working conditions so that the company has a strategy to continually expand its staff. Many firms are using the Internet as a recruiting tool. They have "careers" sections on their Web sites providing general employment information and listing open positions. Internet recruiting is a quick, efficient, inexpensive way to reach a large pool of job seekers at employment Web sites such as Monster.com

---

# Business Plan

## I. Executive Summary
· Who
· What
· When
· Where
· Why
· How

## II. Table of Contents

## III. Introduction
· The concept and the company
· The management team
· The Product

## IV. Marketing Strategy
· Demographics
· Trends
· Market penetration
· Potential sales revenue

## V. Financing the Business
· Cash flow analysis
· Pro forma balance sheet
· Income statement

## VI. Resumes of Principals

---

## Steps in Recruitment and Selection Process

Entrepreneurs and small businesses usually assume most of the responsibility for their Human Resources department, however, a growing number of small firms are outsourcing this function to professional employer organizations (PEO). A PEO is a company that helps firms with a wide range of Human Resources services, including hiring and training employees, administrating payroll and benefits programs, handling worker's compensation and unemployment insurance, and insuring compliance with labor laws. These PEOs work in partnership with employers in these key decisions.[19]

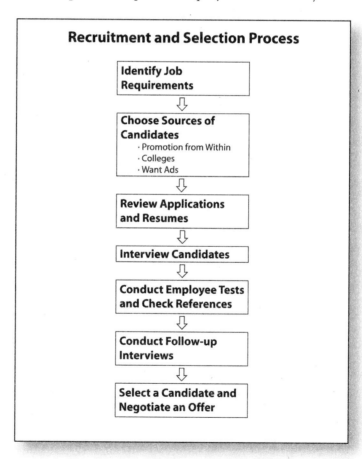

---

[19] Boone, Louis E., David L. and Kurtz. 2006. *Contemporary Business, 2006: Custom Version for Santa Monica College.* 11th ed. Mason: Thomson South-Western. P. 297–300.

## Certifications for Women Entrepreneurs

Certifications are highly recognized by hundreds of major corporations as well as many federal and governmental agencies to help women entrepreneurs grow their businesses. Certifying your company proves that your business is a woman-owned business, and that the business is managed full time by a woman. Your business must be owned and at least 51-percent controlled by one or more women.

You have to invest some time and money in the certification process. You have to be willing to share very sensitive documentation that you are required to present such as taxes, corporate documents, bank statements, balance sheet, and payroll as well as some personal financial information.

My company has been certified for many years now. In current years, I have seen more activity especially with large corporations requiring certification. I have completed the National Women Business Owners Corporation (NBWOC) certification, and I also suggest becoming certified by the Women's Business Enterprise National Council (WBENC) and the National Minority Supplier Development Council (NMSDC). If possible, do them simultaneously. They require almost identical documentation, and it is easier to photocopy one set of papers once you have everything on hand. Each application has a cost but once you are done, you just need to renew them each year. It is much easier just to inform them of any important changes in your business.

My certification has helped me with one of my largest customers: Wal-Mart. Certifications have also brought value to my company over the years.

Here is some information about organizations to which you can apply for certifications:

## National Women Business Owners Corporation

The National Women Business Owners Corporation (NWBOC) has led the way for women business owners to obtain WBE

Certification. Created in 1995, NWBOC was established to increase competition for corporate and government contracts through implementation of a national certification program for women business owners. The development of our national Woman Business Enterprise (WBE) certification program, sponsored by IBM, involved cooperation and input from over seven hundred public- and private-sector individuals. The result was the creation of the WBE Application, the process, and the NWBOC Standards and Procedures.

NWBOC was created in response to needs identified by the Procurement Special Interest Group of the National Association of Women Business Owners (NAWBO). The investigation revealed that to a large degree, corporate America and government agencies had not received, nor recognized, the benefits of contracting with women suppliers. Only a small fraction of corporate and government contracts were with women-owned firms. This mindset prevented purchasers from obtaining the best value in their procurements, and it limited women business owners from penetrating these markets, which has stymied their business growth. Research has shown that after developing supplier partnerships with women-owned firms, many companies and government agencies have enhanced their bottom line for their shareholders and taxpayers, respectively. (www.nwboc.org)

## Women's Business Enterprise National Council

The Women's Business Enterprise National Council (WBENC), founded in 1997, is the nation's leading advocate of women-owned businesses as suppliers to America's corporations. It also is the largest third-party certifier of businesses owned and operated by women in the United States. WBENC works to foster diversity in the world of commerce with programs and policies designed to expand opportunities and eliminate barriers in the marketplace for women business owners. WBENC works with representatives of corporations to encourage the utilization and expansion of supplier/vendor diversity programs.

Dedicated to enhancing opportunities for women's business enterprises, WBENC works in partnership with women's business organizations located throughout the country to provide a national standard of certification for women-owned businesses. The organization also provides its corporate members and certified women's business enterprises (WBEs) with access to a range of B2B sourcing tools including an Internet database—WBENCLink—that contains information on certified women's businesses for purchasing managers nationwide. WBENC is a resource for the more than seven hundred U.S. companies and government agencies that rely on the WBENC certification as an integral part of their supplier diversity programs.

Through its benchmarking surveys and ongoing interaction with certified women's business enterprises, WBENC has become the nation's leading source of information on trends in supplier diversity programs for WBEs at U.S. companies and government agencies. WBENC also promotes best practices in supplier diversity through the annual selection of "America's Top Corporations for Women's Business Enterprises." (www.wbenc.org)

### National Minority Supplier Development Council

Providing a direct link between corporate America and minority-owned businesses is the primary objective of the National Minority Supplier Development Council, one of the country's leading business membership organizations. It was chartered in 1972 to provide increased procurement and business opportunities for minority businesses of all sizes.

The NMSDC Network includes a National Office in New York and thirty-nine regional councils across the country. There are thirty-five hundred corporate members throughout the network, including most of America's largest publicly owned, privately owned, and foreign-owned companies, as well as universities, hospitals, and other buying institutions. The regional councils certify and match more than fifteen thousand minority-owned businesses (Asian, Black, Hispanic, and Native American) with member corporations that want to purchase goods and services.

As for government certifications, they consist of multiple agencies that operate independently of one another, and each one has their own certification process. As you read the stories of our Latinas, you saw very successful contacts like Olga Martinez, Patricia Pliego Stout, and Theresa Daytener with the SBA 8(a) certification. Here is some of the information.

## 8(a) Business-Development Program for the Disadvantaged

The U.S. Small Business Administration (SBA) has a certification process for the 8(a) Business Development Program to assist Small Disadvantaged Businesses (SDB). This program assists in the development of small companies owned and operated by individuals who are socially and economically disadvantaged. The SDB certification ensures that small businesses are owned and controlled by socially and economically disadvantaged individuals meeting SDB eligibility criteria. If you are considered a SDB, you may receive a price evaluation credit of up to 10 percent when you bid on a federal contract. Businesses eligible for this program may receive federal contracting set-asides and other business-development support to help the company gain access to the economic mainstream.

## Small Business Certification Program

The Small Business (SB) Certification Program, a certification I applied for and received in 2007, was established to increase business opportunities for the small-business community within the state of California, thereby stimulating the state's overall economy. The program was designed to help small businesses exist on a more level playing field with certain advantages when competing against other non-small businesses for state contracts and purchases. Certified firms can also take advantage of other small-business benefits.

Every year, each state agency must submit to the legislature an annual report that tracks contract award activity involving SBs. The report must demonstrate that the various participation goals have been met or exceeded. If the minimum goals are not met, the agency must provide a sound justification along with the remedial action they will take to attain or exceed the goal(s) the following year.

The Department of General Services (DGS), Procurement Division (PD), Office of Small Business is the state's certifying agency that administers the Small Business Certification Programs. While small-business and DVBE certification is the OSDS's primary role, they also assist SBs in a variety of ways including conducting outreach events, providing resource guidance, and supporting the businesses through advocacy. (www.pd.dgs.ca.gov/smbus)

## Keeping an Edge as a Latina

I keep an edge as a CEO by communicating with other entrepreneurs, with my mentors, and with my advisors. I have the need to talk things out, and it helps to have someone you trust serving as a sounding board.

I love to attend conferences around the country to meet other CEO's and learn from their experiences, be motivated, and keep going with my own business. Such events have had a big impact in my life, and now this is what I want to do for the next generation of entrepreneurs who are planning to have a business one day. I also volunteer as part of advisory boards at nonprofit organizations or corporations, which is a good way to stay up to date on different industries. The Latina blood in me loves keeping in touch personally and professionally.

## To-Do List: *Lista de Quehaceres*

I constantly write a "To-Do List" for my business and personal projects. Now, why is it that it seems things do not get done as quickly as we want, and what is there to do about it?

These are some examples of obstacles business owners face in action items:

- We are too busy performing the day-to-day tasks in our business to ever get to the long-term strategic tasks.

- We are unclear on how to implement action items.

- We begin working on one task, see something else that needs to be done (even if it is a low priority), and turn our attention to the new task at hand.

- We lose focus. This process generally continues until the end of the day, and when we finally realize that most of the time was taken up by low-priority jobs, we get upset.

- We pick tasks that can be done quickly or that we personally like doing in order to get the feeling of accomplishing something each and every day.

Recommendations

1. Avoid interruptions. This means turning off the phones and closing your door. Arrive earlier to work or stay later at night. We are twice as effective with no distractions.

2. Delegate every task that can be done by someone else in the organization.

3. Do not ignore a problem; not taking action will only lead to frustration.

**4.** You need someone to hold you accountable for your actions. Have someone periodically review you. Having an advisory board, a consultant, or a mentor can keep you right on track.

**5.** Prioritize your list. Do not add more tasks to the list unless you already deleted some of the old projects. Add an estimated date when each project will be done, and make sure that you comply.

Every situation is different; it is vital to the future of the business that you as the business owner address the most important issues, recognize your leadership, and take action.

## What's Next for This Latina?

Now that you are equipped with the necessary information for the formation of a business, the next step you need to consider is how you will finance your business. In the next chapter you will find some of the most common ways people finance their businesses.

# Chapter 10:
# Ideas for Financing

One of the most important issues when starting a business is financing. There are two especially important questions:

1. How much money will you need to start a business?

2. Where are you going to get the money you need?

The requirements for the amount of money you will need depend upon the kind of business you plan to run. Many of the nation's fastest-growing small businesses start with a very limited amount of money. The majority of entrepreneurs rely on personal resources such as savings, friends and family, and credit cards, as well as banks, venture capitalists, angel investors, and different kinds of loans, among other options. All of these resources will be explored briefly in this chapter to help with a process that can sometimes be overwhelming, but in the end, is the most necessary component of starting your own business.

One of the most important parts of running a business is understanding how to read financial statements and cash flow: the way money flows through the company. As soon as you are ready to establish a business, hire a Certified Public Accountant (CPA) who can provide you with the necessary information you will need before you make any mistakes. The routine of budgeting, planning, and looking at your profit and loss (P&L) statements on a regular basis with your accountant will provide vital information.

As you will recall from the stories of the entrepreneurs, all of them started with personal savings, family loans, and credit cards. Only one of them, Liza Roeser Atwood, found a way to start her business with no money at all. While she is the exception to the rule, she also embodies the fact that it can be done as long as you have a strong business reputation upon which to rely. And in the end, all of the women have been extremely successful even though they had very difficult beginnings.

## Financing Latina Style

The primary source for capital for most new businesses comes from savings and other types of personal resources. Many entrepreneurs look to private sources such as friends and family when starting out in a business venture. Often, money is loaned interest-free or at a low interest rate, which can be beneficial when getting started. Don't just ask mom and dad for loans, try other members of your family or close friends who are interested in an investment. But make sure that you are professional and that you keep your word regarding any promises that are made. Providing a written agreement will help keep things professional.[20]

## Credit Cards

These are usually good for quick, short-term loans. According to the SBA, credit cards are one of the most widely used forms of financing by small businesses, despite their usually high interest rates. The heaviest users of credit cards for business financing are tiny firms with fewer than ten employees. This is the case because banks are usually willing to approve someone for a corporate card if they have a good credit record with a consumer credit card.

---

[20] www.sba.gov

And even when an entrepreneur doesn't have great credit, there is a good possibility that they will be approved for a credit card. Do keep in mind, however, that it is very important when considering starting a business to have a good credit score.

## Bank Loans

The owner can also raise capital for a business using an equity loan on her home or other assets she may own. Banks offer loans with varying terms, and usually provide the following types of credit: term loans, real-estate financing, leasing, and lines of credit. There are also non-bank financing options such as life-insurance companies, credit-card firms, commercial-finance companies, and other options. Other options include a partnership with a larger company, a second mortgage on your home, people looking for a share of ownership in return for investing, and community-development loans. Many owners seek a bank loan in the name of their business; however, banks will usually insist upon a personal guarantee by the business owner.

The Small Business Administration (SBA) runs several loan programs that may help a small business secure loans. In these programs, the SBA guarantees a portion of the loan to the issuing bank, thus relieving the bank of some of the risk of extending the loan to a small business. (www.sba.gov)

## Other Types of Business Loans

Terms of loans may vary from lender to lender, but there are two basic types of loans: short-term and long-term. Generally, a short-term loan has a maturity of up to one year. These include working-capital loans, accounts-receivable loans and lines of credit. Long-term loans have maturities greater than one year but usually fewer than seven years. Real-estate and equipment loans may have maturities of up to twenty-five years. Longterm loans are used for major business expenses such as purchasing real estate and facilities, construction, durable equipment, furniture and fixtures, vehicles, etc[21].

## Small Business Administration

SBA loan programs are generally intended to encourage longer-term small-business financing, but actual loan maturities are based on the ability to repay, the purpose of the loan proceeds, and the useful life of the assets financed. However, maximum loan maturities have been established: twenty-five years for real estate; up to ten years for equipment (depending on the useful life of the equipment); and generally up to seven years for working capital. Short-term loans are also available through the SBA to help small businesses meet their short-term and cyclical working-capital needs.

The SBA offers a variety of financing options for small businesses. Whether you are looking for a long-term loan for machinery and equipment, a general working capital loan, a revolving line of credit, or a microloan, the SBA has a financing program to fit your needs.

## SBA Guaranty Loan Program

Your loan-repayment schedule depends on the use of the proceeds and the ability of your business to repay. The general terms are five to ten years for working capital and up to twenty-five years for fixed assets such as the purchase or major renovation of real estate or the purchase of equipment (not to exceed the useful life of the equipment). Both fixed and variable interest rates are available. The interest rate is negotiated between the borrower and the lender/bank. However, lenders generally may not charge over the maximum rate of 2.25 percent over the lowest prime rate for a loan with a maturity of fewer than seven years and 2.75 percent over

---

[21] www.sba.gov

prime for a maturity of seven years or longer. For loans under $50,000, the lender's rate may be slightly higher.

## My SBA Success Story

By 1989 I had never had a loan from any institution. One day my bank suggested that I could qualify for an SBA loan. I had never heard of the SBA. They explained this was a loan with less interest that was guaranteed by the government. I prepared my business plan, and a loan was approved for close to a million dollars to purchase real estate in a 504 program. At the time, that was the maximum amount they guaranteed. This gave me the opportunity to move my company to a whole new level of growth.

## Approval Criteria

The first hurdle to overcome involves a determination by the lender that the borrower is unable to obtain funding from "non-federal sources." Submission of a loan application by a participating lender constitutes certification that it has examined the availability of credit to the applicant and that substantiation of this examination is contained in the borrower's file. In addition, an applicant must show that the desired funds are not available from the personal resources of any owner with 20 percent or more of the equity of the applicant. Such funds must be injected prior to the disbursement of any SBA financing. Liquid assets include cash or cash equivalents such as savings accounts, CDs, stocks, bonds, or other similar assets (excluding equity in real estate and other fixed assets). Once these hurdles are surpassed, three major requirements must be met for a bank (with or without SBA guarantees) to consider approving a business acquisition loan:

1. Strong credit history of owner.

2. Relevant management experience on the part of borrower.

3. Sufficient cash flow to service debt and provide a living wage for borrower.

## Choosing a Lender

When searching for an SBA lender, it is important to do your homework before becoming involved with any particular bank or non-bank lender. It is common for one lender to reject a loan for business-acquisition financing, while another lender approves essentially the same loan. Given the effort, time, and money that go into this process, carefully selecting a lender is one of the most important tasks facing a would-be borrower. To make the right choice, it is important to discuss a given bank's performance in this area with other entrepreneurs who have been through this process. Ask fellow business owners, your CPA, your attorney, and your business broker to obtain feedback on various lenders and the performance of each in providing SBA financing. Business brokers are exceptionally good sources of such information because they are paid only if a deal is funded and closes. Because brokers are not typically paid a referral fee, student-loan obligations, delinquent child support, and unsatisfied liens and adjustments are grounds for refusal. Felony convictions also disqualify a buyer immediately. The relevant management experience tends to be the most flexible requirement of all in that general managerial experience seems to be generally transferable across industries. There are exceptions, but there appears to be great latitude and discretion on the part of the lender in this area.

## Getting a Small-Business Loan

Documentation requirements may vary; contact your lender to learn the information you must supply. Common requirements include: purpose of the loan, history of the business, financial statements for three years (existing businesses), schedule of term debts (existing businesses), aging of accounts receivable and payable (existing businesses), projected opening-day balance sheet (new businesses), lease details, amount of investment in the business by the owner(s), projections of income, expenses and cash flow, signed personal financial statements, and personal résumé(s). Develop a short statement on each principal in your business, and provide background, education, experience, skills, and accomplishments. Clearly define your company's products as well as your markets. Identify your competition and explain how your business competes in the marketplace. Profile your customers and explain how your business can satisfy their needs. In other words, this needs to be supported by your business plan.

You should take the information, including your loan proposal, and submit it to a local lender. If the lender is unable to approve your loan, you may ask if the lender can consider your request under the SBA loan-guaranty program. Under this program, the SBA can guarantee up to 85 percent of a small-business loan; however, the lender must agree to loan the money with the SBA guarantee. That means the business owner must be prepared to come up with at least the other 15 percent of the loan. You must be prepared to pledge collateral as security for the loan.

The lender will then forward your loan application and a credit analysis to the nearest SBA district office. After receiving all documentation, the SBA analyzes the entire application, then makes its decision. The length of the process varies. If the lender needs SBA applications and/or guidance, it may contact the nearest SBA district office by visiting http://www.sba.gov/localresources/index.html. Upon SBA approval, the lending institution closes the loan and disburses the funds. To be eligible, a business must be operated for profit and not exceed SBA's size standards.

## Writing a Loan Proposal

Approval of your loan request depends on how well you present yourself, your business, and your financial needs to a lender. Remember, lenders want to make loans, but they must make loans they know will be repaid. The best way to improve your chances of obtaining a loan is to prepare a written proposal. One very valuable resource when you are filling out an SBA loan application is SCORE, the Service Corps of Retired Executives (www.score.org). They are volunteers who share business advice based on their business experience.

## Investment Capital

The owner can finance a business by getting investors to purchase stock in the company. A partnership can be formed or perhaps a venture capitalist could provide funds if the business venture plans were sound enough. The owner should realize that if anyone else participates in the venture, some elements of control will be lost. All investors should be aware of the risks involved when one invests in a start-up business[22].

## Venture Capitalists

These firms help expanding companies grow in exchange for equity or partial ownership. VCs are an entirely different breed from angel investors. While angel investors are private individuals, venture capitalists are full-fledged partnerships and companies devoted to start-up and small company funding. They can range in size from tens to hundreds of people and can command multi-millions in annual funding. When dealing with venture capitalists, one needs to understand that like their namesake, they are "capitalists." VC firms survive and profit from making investments in companies that pay back in multiple returns over the long run. VC firms take their investments seriously, so be prepared to be closely scrutinized. Of course, the payoff is sweeter with initial funding from a few hundred thousand dollars up and further investments in the millions.[23]

The drawbacks of VCs are as follow: "VCs typically only invest in established companies. You must be willing to give up significant control over major decisions for your company, but there are ways

---

[22] www.smallbusiness.com
[23] www.teenanalyst.com

that you can negotiate that before you make the final decision. You must be ready to partner with and have an aggressive exit strategy to sell your business or do an Initial Public Offering (IPO) within 5–7 years.[24] (startupnation.com)

## Angel Investors

Angel investors are wealthy individuals willing to invest money directly in new ventures for equity stakes. They invest more capital in start-ups than venture capitalists. Angels focus primarily on new ventures and are an option when you need anywhere between $250,000 and $750,000 in capital. While angel investors are primarily looking for a positive return on their money, meaning they hope to earn at least their initial investment back over time, they typically are laxer on this issue than corporate backers. Some angel investors are simply wealthy individuals who enjoy helping bring a good idea to fruition. An angel investor usually works in close contact with the start-up company and can provide some personal attention to the job of building a business team, which is always good.[25]

## Mergers and Acquisitions

In a merger, two or more firms combine to form one company; in an acquisition, one firm purchases the property and assumes the obligations of another. Acquisitions also occur when one firm buys a division or subsidiary from another firm. Many mergers and acquisitions cross national borders, as managers attempt to enter new markets and improve global competitiveness for their companies.

## Joint Ventures

A joint venture is a partnership between companies formed for a specific undertaking. Sometimes a company enters into a joint

---

[24] www.startupnation.com
[25] www.teenanalyst.com

venture with a local firm or government, sharing the operation costs, risk management, and profits with its local partner.

This chapter has outlined the many options available for financing. All of the women in the book used one form or another of the ideas for finding financing suggested in this chapter, and they have all done well for themselves. In the next chapter, I will introduce you to the concept of branding.

# Chapter 11:
# Branding Concepts You Should Know First

Branding is the process of creating an identity in consumers' minds for a good, service, or company. It is an important tool used by marketing-oriented companies.

A brand name is the part of the brand consisting of words or letters included in a name, used to identify and distinguish the firm's offerings from those of competitors. The brand name is the part of the brand that can be vocalized. A brand can be a name, term, sign, symbol, design, or some combination of these that identifies the products of one firm and differentiates them from competitors' offerings.

THE ALAMO TRAVEL GROUP, INC.

Good brands are easy to pronounce, recognize and remember: Crest, Visa, and Avis are examples. Global firms face a real problem in selecting brand names, since an excellent brand name in one country may prove disastrous in another. Brand names should also convey the right image to the buyer.

Brand names must also be legally protectable. Trademark law specifies that brand names cannot contain words in general use, such as "television" or "automobile." Generic words—words that describe a type of product—cannot be used exclusively by any organization. On the other hand, if a brand name becomes so popular that it passes into common language and becomes a generic word, the company can no longer use it as a brand name. Once upon a time, aspirin, linoleum, and zipper were exclusive brand names, but today, they have become generic terms and are no longer legally protected.

A trademark is a brand that has been given legal protection. The protection is granted solely to the brand's owner. Trademark protection includes not only the brand name, but also design logos, slogans, packaging elements, and product features such as color and shape. A well-designed trademark can make a definite difference in how consumers perceive a brand.[26]

---

[26] Boone, Louis E., David L. and Kurtz. 2006. *Contemporary Business, 2006: Custom Version for Santa Monica College.* 11th ed. Mason: Thomson South-Western. P. 15, 427–29.

## Brand Categories

### Brand Loyalty

Marketers measure brand loyalty in three stages: brand recognition, brand preference, and brand insistence. *Brand Recognition* is brand acceptance strong enough that the consumer is aware of the brand, but not strong enough to cause a preference over other brands. Advertising, free samples, and discount coupons are among the most common ways to increase brand recognition.

### Brand Preference

Brand preference occurs when a consumer chooses one firm's brand over a competitor's. At this stage, the consumer is usually relying on previous experience in selecting the product. Automobiles and apparel fall into this category. Eight of ten owners of a Mercedes-Benz choose that brand again when they buy a new car.

### Brand Insistence

Brand insistence is the ultimate degree of brand loyalty, in which the consumer will accept no substitute for a preferred brand. If the desired product is not available, the consumer will look for it at another outlet, special-order it from a dealer, order by mail, or search the Internet.

### Brand Equity

Brand loyalty is the heart of brand equity, the added value that a widely respected, highly successful name gives to a product in the marketplace. This value results from a combination of factors including awareness, loyalty, and perceived quality, as well as any feelings or images the customer associates with the brand. High brand equity offers financial advantages to a firm since the product commands a relatively large market share and sometimes reduces price sensitivity, generating higher profits. The world's five most valuable brands include Coca-Cola, Microsoft, IBM, Intel and Nokia.

"Branding is far too important to be left to the marketing department. It's everyone's responsibility, but most of all, the brand champion of the company must be the company's leader—whether you call yourself CEO, president, or founder, you will set the tone for the brand because only you touch every area of the corporation. If you are a brand champion, you will ensure that it is incorporated into every department, every initiative"(BQ, xiii) These words come from *What's Your BQ*, a recent book by branding expert Sandra Sellani. She also graciously contributed the following valuable information:

### Thinking of Starting a Business? Five Branding Concepts You Should Know First by Sandra Sellani

1. Before you spend a cent on any branding, make sure that what you are offering is unique compared to your competitors. Use the VRIO model—your offering must be Valuable, Rare, difficult to Imitate and you must build the Organization around this point of differentiation.

2. Don't associate good branding with spending a lot of money. Make a budget and stick to it. Some of the best campaigns begin with a simple tagline. The tagline gives people an instant snapshot of what your brand represents.

3. Be smart about PR. Public relations can provide a huge brand boost, but know how to appeal to the media.

4. Beware of people trying to sell advertising space to you. Many ad reps will try to sell you space that will not benefit your company in any way. They're trying to make a buck, but don't fall prey to it. Know your target audience. Know what they read. Know how they make decisions. In some cases, a small $100 ad in a local newspaper will get you more business than a $2,000 ad in a publication that your clients don't read.

**5.** Keep your finger on the pulse of your clients, prospects, and competitors. Once your brand becomes successful, competitors will imitate your offering—and if they do a better job of selling your idea than you do, you may lose clients and prospects to these imitators.

Now that you know a little about branding, you should be aware of its importance. The following chapter will give you information about marketing.

# Chapter 12:
# What Marketing Is all About

Let's start talking about one of the most important areas of the business: Marketing.

## Marketing Basics

To succeed, entrepreneurs must attract and retain a growing base of satisfied customers. Marketing programs, though widely varied, are all aimed at convincing people to try or keep using particular products or services. Business owners should carefully plan their marketing strategies and performance to keep their market presence strong.

## What Is Marketing?

Marketing is based on the importance of customers to a business and has two important principles:

- All company policies and activities should be directed toward satisfying customer needs.

- Profitable sales volume is more important than maximum sales volume.

To best use these principles, a small business should:

- Determine the needs of their customers through market research.
- Analyze their competitive advantages to develop a market strategy.
- Select specific markets to serve by target marketing.
- Determine how to satisfy customer needs by identifying a market mix.

## Market Research

Successful marketing requires timely and relevant market information. An inexpensive research program based on questionnaires given to current or prospective customers can often uncover dissatisfaction or possible new products or services.

Market research will also identify trends that affect sales and profitability. Population shifts, legal developments, and the local economic situation should be monitored to quickly identify problems and opportunities. It is also important to keep up with competitors' market strategies.

## Marketing Strategy

A marketing strategy identifies customer groups that a particular business can better serve than its target competitors, tailoring product offerings, prices, distribution, promotional efforts, and services toward those consumers. Ideally, the strategy should address unmet customer needs that offer adequate potential profitability. A good strategy helps a business focus on the target markets it can serve best.

## Target Marketing

Owners of small businesses usually have limited resources to spend on marketing. Concentrating their efforts on one or a few key market segments—target marketing—gets the most return from small investments. There are two methods used to segment a market:

**Geographical Segmentation:** Specializing in serving the needs of customers in a particular geographical area. For example, a neighborhood convenience store may send advertisements only to people living within one-half mile of the store.

**Customer Segmentation:** Identifying those people most likely to buy the product or service and targeting those groups.

## Managing the Market Mix

Every marketing program contains four key components; products and services, promotion, distribution, and pricing.

**Products and Services:** Product strategies may include concentrating on a narrow product line, developing a highly specialized product or service, or providing a product-service package containing unusually high-quality service.

**Promotion:** Promotion strategies include advertising and direct customer interaction. Good salesmanship is essential for small businesses because of their limited ability to spend on advertising. Good telephone-book advertising is also important. Direct mail is an effective, low-cost medium available to small business.

**Price:** The right price is crucial for maximizing total revenue. Generally, higher prices mean lower volume and vice versa; however, small businesses can often command higher prices because of their personalized service.

**Distribution:** The manufacturer and wholesaler must decide how to distribute their products. Working through established distributors or manufacturers' agents is generally easiest for small manufacturers. Small retailers should consider cost and traffic flow in site selection, especially since advertising and rent can be reciprocal: A low-cost, low-traffic location means spending more on advertising to build traffic.

These all combine into an overall marketing program.

The nature of the product or service is also important in citing decisions. If purchases are based largely on impulse, then high traffic and visibility are critical. On the other hand, location is less of a concern for products or services that customers are willing to go out of their way to find. The recent availability of highly segmented mailing lists, purchased from list brokers, magazines, or other companies, has enabled certain small businesses to operate from any location, yet serve national or international markets.

## Marketing Performance

After implementing a marketing program, entrepreneurs must evaluate its performance. Every program should have performance standards to compare with actual results. Researching industry norms and past performances will help to develop appropriate standards.

Entrepreneurs should audit their company's performance at least quarterly. The key questions are:

- Is the company doing all it can to be customer-oriented?

- Do employees ensure the customers are satisfied and leave wanting to come back?

- Is it easy for the customer to find what he or she wants at a competitive price?

## Marketing Plans

A sound marketing plan is key to the success of your business. It should include your market research, location, the customer group you have targeted, competition, positioning, the product or service you are selling, pricing, advertising, and promotion.

Effective marketing, planning, and promotion begin with current information about the marketplace. Visit your local library, talk to customers, study the advertising of other businesses in your community, and consult with any relevant industry associations. This interactive tool will help you assess your marketing strengths and weaknesses.

Once you have all the necessary information, write down your plan:

1. **Define your business:**

   - Your product or service

   - Your geographic marketing area: neighborhood, regional, or national

   - Your competition

   - How you differ from the competition—what makes you special

   - Your price

   - The competition's promotion methods

   - Your promotion methods

   - Your distribution methods or business location

2. **Define your customers:**

   - Your current customer base: age, gender, income, and neighborhood

   - How your customers learn about your product or service: advertising, direct mail, word of mouth, Yellow Pages

   - Patterns or habits your customers and potential customers share: where they shop; what they read, watch, and listen to

   - Qualities your customers value most about your product or service: selection, convenience, service, reliability, availability, and affordability

   - Qualities your customers like least about your product or service: Can they be adjusted to serve your customers better?, prospective customers whom you aren't currently reaching

### 3. Define your plan and budget:

- Previous marketing methods you have used to communicate to your customers
- Methods that have been most effective
- Cost compared to sales
- Cost per customer
- Possible future marketing methods to attract new customers
- Percentage of profits you can allocate to your marketing campaign
- Marketing tools you can implement within your budget: newspaper, magazine, Yellow Pages, radio or television advertising, direct mail, telemarketing, and public-relations activities such as community involvement, sponsorship, or press releases
- Methods of testing your marketing ideas
- Methods for measuring results of your marketing campaign
- The marketing tool you can implement immediately

The final component in your marketing plan should be your overall promotional objectives: to communicate your message, create an awareness of your product or service, motivate customers to buy and increase sales, or other specific targets. Objectives make it easier to design an effective campaign and help you keep that campaign on the right track. Once you have defined your objectives, it is easier to choose the method that will be most effective.

## Establishing a Web Presence

A business Web site can be a virtual marketing brochure that you can update on demand with little or no cost. Your presence on the Internet can be a useful marketing tool by providing richer presale information or post-sale support and service. This might temporarily differentiate your product or service from that of your competitors.

E-marketing has lessened the disadvantage that small businesses have faced for years when competing with larger businesses.

E-commerce has redefined the marketplace, altered business strategies, and allowed global competition between local businesses. The term "electronic commerce" has evolved from meaning simply electronic shopping to representing all aspects of business and market processes enabled by the Internet and other digital technologies. The SBA is preparing to help this new generation of Internet-enabled or e-Small Businesses.

Today's business emphasis is on e-commerce: rapid electronic interactions enabled by the Internet and other connected computer and telephone networks. Rapid business transactions and unparalleled access to information is changing consumer behavior and expectations. The U.S. Small Business Administration (SBA) is reshaping its programs to better serve small businesses that take advantage of the Internet and other emerging technologies.[27]

## Public Relations

Just as the best marketing is targeted, likewise the best P.R. is segmented to promote a business' key strengths to select audiences with specific messaging and timing. Public Relations "refers to an organization's nonpaid communications with its various public audiences, such as customers, vendors, news media, employees, stockholders, the government, and the general public."[28] It can be as important to a company's marketing effort as its advertising.

Public Relations is an efficient, indirect communications channel for promoting products, services, and brands. It can publicize products and help to create and maintain a positive image of the company. The PR department links a firm with the media. It provides the media with news releases, video and audio clips, as well as holding news

---

[27] www.sba.gov
[28] Boone, Louis E., David L. and Kurtz. 2006. *Contemporary Business, 2006: Custom Version for Santa Monica College.* 11th ed. Mason: Thomson South-Western. P. 468–469.

conferences to announce new products, the formation of strategic alliances, management changes, financial results, and similar developments. Publications issued by the PR department include newsletters, brochures and reports.

Public Relations enhances product or company credibility and creates a positive attitude about the product or the company. I have dedicated a great deal of time in my career to expanding my Public Relations and branding my company. It is one of the areas that I like to work with the most not only for the connections and people that I have met, but also because I am in continuous communication with my customers. It is very important to take the time and visit your customers at least once a year.

Public relations has also taken me to the next level of public speaking and this has been a great tool to share not only my story but to keep my brand in front of so many thousands of people, while at the same time getting media attention. I have to share that at the beginning, I was very afraid of speaking in public and as the years went by, I have trained myself by watching other speakers and improving my skills. Now I really enjoy speaking with my accent. I am so very proud and not even shy when I am on a stage; I love it!

Below are some of my personal network strategies.

## Lulu's Networking Strategies

1. Effective networking involves a commitment of time, energy, and resources that produce meaningful results.

2. Choose the right networking group or event, e.g., tradeshows, conferences, associations.

3. Focus on quality contacts vs. quantity: two to five good new contacts for each networking meeting.

4. Make a positive first impression. You have ONE opportunity to make a great first impression. Approach people with a natural, genuine smile, listen carefully to their name, ask

them to repeat if you didn't understand it. Important factors are: handshake, facial expressions, eye contact, listening skills.

5. Make a powerful impression by asking them what they do before talking about yourself.

6. Give and get information. Cover these topics:

   • What does your company do?
   • What type of clients do you serve?
   • Who makes the buying decision for you?
   • What sets you apart from your competition?

7. Network for management ideas, advice, leads, even vendor recommendations.

8. Be careful to never burn bridges; you never know when someone will be able to help you.

9. Keep your records organized and follow up after the event by e-mail, phone calls, and visits.

10. Remember clients' birthdays, and acknowledge important achievements or a favorite hobby or sports team. The fact that you are thinking about the client will pay huge dividends.

11. Build trust and confidence in your leadership ability and work ethic by providing excellence in your business.

### Enterprising Women Exhibit: One of Few Latinas

In October 2002, I was given some very exciting news. I was told I would be featured in *Enterprising Women: 250 Years of American Business,* organized by the Schlesinger Library of the Radcliffe Institute for Advanced Study at Harvard University and the National Heritage Museum in Lexington, Massachusetts. It is an exhibition that "brings to life the stories of some 40 intriguing women who helped shape the landscape of American business." Organized into five historic sections and enhanced by interactive and evocative settings, such as an 18th-century print shop, a 19th-century dressmaking shop, a turn-of-the-century beauty parlor, and a 20th-century corporate office, *Enterprising Women* illuminates and personalizes the nation's transformation from an agricultural and household economy to one influenced by industrialization, the rise of big business, the emergence of consumer culture, and the technology revolution. I couldn't believe I would be featured along with some of the most accomplished women in the history of the U.S. From the 20th century there were such women represented as Oprah, Martha Stewart, and Meg Whitman. Entrepreneurship has become the path to prosperity for many Americans, especially minorities and women. It was an amazing honor to be included in this exhibition. You can find more information online at http://www.radcliffe.edu/schles/exhibits/enterprisingwomen.

For all of the women in this book, marketing has been a very important aspect of their business. From developing logos to Web sites to business cards to labels, marketing is the second most important department after financing because it eventually leads to sales. Visiting clients and promoting at shows is necessary, but the most important part of marketing is to have personal contact with the customers. Now that you know what marketing is all about, you will find next a very important chapter for the development or betterment of your company: "Valuable Resources for Latinas."

# Chapter 13:
# Valuable Resources for Latinas

Now that you've become familiarized with the most important aspects of a business from establishing it, to financing, to branding, to marketing, there is one more aspect to explore. As the title of the chapter suggests, this chapter delves into resources that I have found very valuable in building my business. While some of the resources may be situated locally, at least it will be helpful to learn that programs such as these exist. I am privileged to belong to some of the organizations, but they are all great programs and entities that will aid you in establishing or improving your business.

## Advisory Boards

An Advisory Board is a nonofficial group of advisors; it has no legal authority or obligation. I have had an advisory board for the last ten years that has helped tremendously in helping me make decisions for my company. I also participate in several advisory boards for different national and international industries to keep myself informed about what is going on in the community. Some of the boards I belong to are: NAWBO-LA, Nacional Financiera, in Mexico, Rancho Santiago Community College Foundation, *Latina*

*Style* Magazine, and many others. Here is a little more information about one of the boards on which I sit: NAFIN.

## Nacional Financiera (NAFIN)

Nacional Financiera, is a Development Banking Institution that operates in accordance with the rules of its own Organic Law, in accordance with the Law of Credit Institutions, and the rules issued by the National Banking Securities (NBSC). The objectives of NAFIN are to promote the overall development and modernization of the industrial sector with a regional approach, stimulate the development of financial markets, and act as financial agent of the federal government in the negotiation, contracting, and management of credits from abroad.

NAFIN carries out its operations in accordance with financing criteria applicable to development banks, channeling its funds mainly through commercial banks and non-banking financial intermediaries. The principal sources of NAFIN's resources are loans from international-development institutions such as the International Bank for Reconstruction and Development (IBRD) and the Inter-American Development Bank (IDB), lines of credit from foreign banks, and the placement of securities in the international and domestic markets. (www.nafin.com)

C.P. Mario Laborin Gomez, President of NAFIN is building bridges between two countries, the U.S. and Mexico. He takes the time to visit personally during board meetings and he has developed a group of 540 "Consejeros Consultivos" throughout the Mexican Republic with three chapters in the U.S. providing financing, technical assistance, and training to small businesses in Mexico.

Being part of the Nacional Financiera Advisory board in Los Angeles has been a great pleasure for me. During my visits to Mexico City, I have been given the opportunity to meet former President Vicente Fox, President Felipe Calderon, and Mexican business owners. The chair of the Los Angeles Chapter, Fernando Niebla, is always looking to expand our relationships in meeting new companies and trying to bring investors into Mexico, as well as receiving the latest reports of financial and political information from around the country.

## Mentors

Mentors can come in so many different forms. My parents were my first mentors. However, you do not even need to know your mentors personally. I remember that when I was younger, I very much admired then-First Lady Jacqueline Kennedy. I followed her life in the news and by reading her books. Another mentor I still have is one of my teachers, Sister Theresa Maksym, whom I have admired for forty years. I have been very fortunate to have found many mentors in my business career who have helped me tremendously in my journey. Find yourself a mentor and have frequent conversations in which you ask the right questions.

## SCORE

The first great resource available I'd like to mention is an organization called SCORE Counselors to America's Small Business. SCORE is America's premier source of free and confidential small-business advice for entrepreneurs. It is a resource partner with the SBA. Headquartered in Herndon, Virginia, and Washington, D.C., SCORE is a 501(c)(3) nonprofit organization dedicated to the formation, growth, and success of small businesses nationwide. Formed in 1964, SCORE provides a public service to America by offering small-business advice and training. SCORE offers face-to-face small-business counseling at 389 chapter offices, where they offer low-cost workshops.

SCORE's 10,500 volunteer counselors have more than 600 business skills. Volunteers are working or retired business owners, executives, and corporate leaders who share their wisdom and lessons learned in business. SCORE Counselors to America's Small Business is a nonprofit association dedicated to entrepreneur education and the formation, growth, and success of small-businesses nationwide. SCORE is a resource partner with the U.S. Small Business Administration.[29] They can be found at www.score.org.

## LATINA *Style* Business Series

The LATINA *Style* Business Series is an interactive business-development program that brings together Latina business owners with key corporations and government agencies that provide the goods and services needed by these outstanding entrepreneurs to create or expand their businesses. Over 10,000 Latina entrepreneurs have participated in the Business Series since its inception in 1998 with the guidance of the U.S. Small Business Administration.

**Target Audience:** Participants are Latina business owners seeking to grow their business and Latina professionals interested in starting a business. Each event typically attracts 200–300 attendees.

**Demographics:** Hispanic-owned business is the fastest-growing segment of the business community. Between 1987 and 1992, these businesses grew at a rate of more than 76 percent, compared with a 26-percent growth rate for all firms. The total revenue for Hispanic-owned businesses increased by 134 percent. According to the U.S. Department of Labor, female Latinas are the fastest-growing small-business owners in the U.S. with a phenomenal growth rate of 114 percent over the last five years. Latinas control 39 percent of the 1.4 million companies owned by women of color in the United States, which generate nearly $147 billion in sales, according to the Center for Business Women's Research. More than one-third (34.9 percent) of all Hispanic businesses are owned by women.

---

[29] www.score.org

**The Program:** The program emphasis is in creating a solid business foundation for the Latina entrepreneur. Corporate sponsors will sponsor an expert panelist or will provide a representative to speak about a specific category of expertise. The program covers a wide-range of topics including: access to capital, strategic sales-and-marketing strategies, professional services, technology, communications, and corporate-and-federal procurement opportunities.

The seminar is a one-day event that includes an exhibit area with a networking breakfast, interactive panel sessions, guest speakers, a Latina entrepreneur award luncheon with a dynamic keynote speaker and closing with a sponsors raffle and dessert reception. (www.latinastyle.com)

## The Office of Small Business Development Centers

The U.S Small Business Administration (SBA) administers the Small Business Development Center Program to provide management assistance to current and prospective small-business owners. SBDCs offer one-stop assistance to individuals and small businesses by providing a wide variety of information and guidance in central and easily accessible branch locations.

The program is a cooperative effort of the private sector, the educational community, and federal, state, and local governments. It enhances economic development by providing small businesses with management and technical assistance.

There are now sixty-three Small Business Development Centers (SBDCs)—one in every state, the District of Columbia, Guam, Puerto Rico, Samoa, and the U.S. Virgin Islands—with a network of more than 1,100 service locations. In each state there is a lead organization that sponsors the SBDC and manages the program. The lead organization coordinates program services offered to small businesses through a network of subcenters and satellite locations. Subcenters are located at colleges, universities, community colleges, vocational schools, chambers of commerce, and economic-development corporations.

SBDC assistance is tailored to the local community and the needs of individual clients. Each center develops services in cooperation with local SBA district offices to ensure statewide coordination with other available resources. Each center has a director, staff members, volunteers, and part-time personnel. Qualified individuals recruited from professional and trade associations, the legal and banking community, academia, chambers of commerce, and SCORE are among those who donate their services. SBDCs also use paid consultants, consulting engineers, and testing laboratories from the private sector to help clients who need specialized expertise.

## What the Program Does:

The SBDC program is designed to deliver up-to-date counseling, training, and technical assistance in all aspects of small-business management. SBDC services include, but are not limited to, assisting small businesses with financial, marketing, production, organization, engineering and technical problems, and feasibility studies. Special SBDC programs and economic-development activities include international trade assistance, technical assistance, procurement assistance, venture-capital formation, and rural development. The SBDCs also make special efforts to reach minority members of socially and economically disadvantaged groups, veterans, women, and the disabled. Assistance is provided to both current or potential small-business owners. They also provide assistance to small businesses applying for Small Business Innovation and Research (SBIR) grants from federal agencies.

## Eligibility:

Assistance from an SBDC is available to anyone interested in starting up a small business for the first time or improving or expanding an existing small business, who cannot afford the services of a private consultant.

## Additional Information:

In addition to the SBDC Program, the SBA provides a variety of other programs and services, including training and educational programs, advisory services, publications, financial programs, and contract assistance. The agency also offers specialized programs for women business owners, minorities, veterans, international trade, and rural development.

The SBA has offices located throughout the country. For the one nearest you, consult the telephone directory under "U.S. Government," or call the Small Business Answer Desk at 1-800-8-ASK-SBA.[30]

## Institute for Women Entrepreneurs

This service provides women with expert and technical assistance to start and grow a business, and also provides resources, mentoring, support, and assistance uniquely tailored to women's needs. These institutions give free and low-cost classes. I am a member of the advisory board for the Orange County Institute for Women Entrepreneurs in Santa Ana, California. The institute in Orange County is funded in part by the SBA and Rancho Santiago Community College District (RSCCD). You can visit their Web site at www.ociwe.org to find out about their classes offered in English, Spanish, and Vietnamese. The Director, Sally Salinas provided the following information:

## What Trends Are and Why Businesses Should Respond to Them

A valuable resource critical to business, yet overlooked, is the information and statistical data found in trends. A trend is the general direction in which something tends to move. It serves as

---

[30] www.sba.gov

an indicator to potential markets and is a valuable tool in responding and executing business strategy and keeping ahead of competition.

Corporations utilize trends and market research for strategic planning, marketing, expansion, and exit strategies. However, it is equally important for the small-business owner to incorporate this type of research into their business plans. Simply put, trends greatly impact business!

The most common questions I receive from my clients are "What types of trends are important?" and "What impact does it have on my business?"

The answer is simple. All businesses must position themselves to succeed, remain competitive, and sustain over time.

Trends are not as difficult to follow as one would think. With the World Wide Web and search engines, pertinent statistics are at your fingertips. There are many types of trends a business could follow. Economic, employment, technological, growth, and demographic trends are just a few.

I advise my clients that understanding demographic trends is critical to keeping their business aligned to the current environment. For example, a significant demographic trend playing out today is the growing number of baby boomers. The U.S. census reflects that in 2006, the oldest of the baby boomers (the generation born between 1946 and 1964) will turn sixty years old. The changing face of the population has created an opportunity for entrepreneurs and businesses to capitalize and serve this demographic.

The possibilities are endless for products and services designed exclusively for mature skin, entertainment, retirement facilities, recreation activities, and so on. Businesses that have not foreca-sted this change in demographics will lag behind those who have responded to it.

Research also indicates that by 2007, one person out of every six will be of Hispanic origin. This emergence has created an explosive market! Businesses that follow and respond to this demographic shift will position themselves for market penetration. I advise all my clients, new and existing, to evaluate their business plan to incorporate strategic opportunities that present themselves through data regarding: food, services, entertainment, international trade, manufacturing, and media that either directly or indirectly address the unique needs of this growing population.

The ability of entrepreneurs to recognize opportunity and strategically respond will have a profound impact on whether or not their business remains competitive and profitable. Small businesses create between 60 and 80 percent of new jobs in America and produce a vibrant economy. There are credible online resources to assist in gathering relevant data to develop a marketing strategy that will position you for market growth and success.

There are over one hundred Women Business Centers around the country, with different names. To find more information, visit www.sba.gov.

### National Hispanic Business Women Association

The National Hispanic Business Women Association is a nonprofit, volunteer-driven business organization whose mission statement is, "To encourage women to develop their business and professional endeavors by promoting business growth through education, mutual support, the sharing of information, business referrals and networking." Its purpose is to develop funding for direct distribution of educational scholarships for students facing financial difficulties, and to develop activities and programs such as business seminars that will help advance and enhance the growth of small businesses and minority-owned businesses. It is located in Orange County, California, and I am privileged to be part of their Advisory Board. (www.nationalhbwa.org)

## National Business Incubation Association

**The National Business Incubation Association** (NBIA) is the world's leading organization advancing business incubation and entrepreneurship. It provides thousands of professionals with the information, education, advocacy, and networking resources to bring excellence to the process of assisting early-stage companies worldwide.

The association is composed primarily of incubator developers and managers; however, technology-commercialization specialists, educators, and business-assistance professionals are also well-represented. Its mission is to provide training and a clearinghouse for information on incubator management and development issues and on tools for assisting start-ups and fledgling firms.

Throughout the year, NBIA offers development activities and specialized training to help business-assistance professionals create and administer effective incubation programs. NBIA also conducts research, compiles statistics, and produces publications that provide a hands-on approach to developing and managing effective programs. In addition, the association tracks relevant legislative initiatives and maintains a speakers' bureau and referral service. It creates partnerships with leading private-sector and public-sector entities to further the interests of the industry and its members.

The National Business Incubation Association is a private, non-profit 501(c)(3) membership organization based in Athens, Ohio. An elected, fifteen-member voting board of directors representing the world's leading incubators governs the association.

Business incubation is a business support process that accelerates the successful development of fledgling companies by providing entrepreneurs with an array of targeted resources and services. These services are usually developed or orchestrated by incubator management and are offered both in the business incubator and through its network of contacts. A business incubator's main goal is to produce successful firms that will leave the program financially viable and freestanding. These incubator graduates have the potential to create jobs, revitalize neighborhoods, commercialize new technologies, and strengthen local and national economies.

Critical to the definition of an incubator is the provision of management guidance, technical assistance, and consulting tailored to burgeoning companies. Incubators usually also provide clients access to appropriate rental space and flexible leases, shared basic business services and equipment, technology-support services, and assistance in obtaining the financing necessary for company growth.

Incubators vary in the way they deliver their services, in their organizational structure, and in the types of clients they serve. Highly adaptable, incubators set goals, including diversifying rural economies, providing employment for and increasing the wealth of depressed inner cities. Incubator clients are at the forefront of developing new and innovative technologies-creating products and services that improve the quality of our lives in communities around the world.

The earliest incubation programs focused on a variety of technology companies or on a combination of light industrial, technology, and service firms are today referred to as mixed-use incubators. However, in more recent years, new incubators have emerged targeting industries such as food processing, medical technology, space technology, ceramics technology, arts and crafts, and software development. Incubator sponsors have also targeted programs to support micro-enterprise creation, the needs of women and minorities, environmental endeavors, and telecommunications. (www.nbia.org)

## The Digital Media Center

The Digital Media Center (DMC), the only facility of its kind in Orange County, California, incorporates specialized college programs and seminars in digital media arts, digital music, TV/video, and business with a business incubator program that nurtures start-up digital-media companies. The Digital Media Center is part of the Rancho Santiago Community College District.

## Requirements

I had the opportunity to visit the Digital Media Center and was amazed by the modern facilities and state-of-the art technology housed there. To be considered as a business incubator resident, your company must submit an executive summary of your business plan to the DMC.

Upon review of your executive summary, you may be asked to provide documentation for some or all of the following admission requirements established by the DMC advisory group. Companies who are in direct competition with a current resident will not be considered for the business incubator program. The following are the requirements for digital- and technology-based companies:

- Provide a realistic business and marketing plan (with specifics regarding product, niche, competitive advantage, management team, staffing, etc.).

- Present financial documentation (income-tax return, credit report, etc.) demonstrating your credit standing. You should have an adequate financial reserve to sustain your business for at least six months.

- Provide the name(s) and position(s) of every full-time employee working in your company.

- Outline how your company will benefit from the services and resources housed within the incubator program and surrounding community.

- Develop a product or service representing a unique technology that can create a competitive advantage.

- Confirm that you have no legal claims or lawsuits pending against your business.

- Outline the potential for job creation at wages higher than the county average.

- Provide a graduation strategy from the DMC that includes a relocation plan to somewhere in the surrounding area.

- Demonstrate a desire to be coached and mentored. (www.dmc-works.com)

## National Association of Women Business Owners

National Association of Women Business Owners® (NAWBO®) is the voice of America's 10.6 million women-owned businesses. Since 1975, NAWBO has strived to propel women entrepreneurs into economic, social, and political spheres of power by: *strengthening* the wealth-creating capacity of our members and promoting economic development within the entrepreneurial community; *creating* innovative and effective changes in the business culture; *building* strategic alliances, coalitions, and affiliations; and *transforming* public policy and influencing opinion makers. National Association of Women Business Owners is the only dues-based national organization representing the interests of all women entrepreneurs across all industries.

Today the organization features chapters in almost every metropolitan area in the United States. By combining the knowledge, networks, and expertise of its diverse membership, board of directors, and staff, NAWBO's strength comes from the diversity of its membership. Businesses range in size from sole proprietorship to hundreds of employees. Members hail from every business industry, from construction and importers, to retailers and service providers, and represent all areas of the country. Membership is open to sole proprietors, partners, and corporate owners with day-to-day management responsibility. Active members who live in a chapter area automatically join both their local chapter and the national chapter. There is also an At-Large Chapter for women business owners outside the chapter areas. (www.nawbo.org)

Since its foundation in 1979, the Los Angeles Chapter of NAWBO (NAWBO-LA) is one of the organization's leading and innovative chapters. NAWBO-LA membership offers women business owners the opportunity to tap into the power of an already-established community of women entrepreneurs. The organization focuses on providing **resources** to help women business owners navigate the different phases of business growth; an **investment** in a total portfolio of personal and professional growth; an **integrated** approach designed for a woman, a business owner, and a leader of the community; and **one voice** that translates into a public policy force to be reckoned with, a formidable economic force and a more effective agent for change in the business environment. Being an active member of NAWBO-LA has proven to be an extremely important business decision for me and my company. As a longstanding member and a current member of its Board of Directors, my participation and engagement with NAWBO-LA has opened doors to new and extraordinary development opportunities. I have traveled to many chapters across the country as a keynote speaker, have been honored at the chapter's Annual Leadership & Legacy Awards Luncheon as "Employer of the Year," have been inducted into the NAWBO-LA Hall of Fame, and have participated in their PEAK Leadership Academy. In May of 2007, I represented NAWBO-LA as part of a delegation of small-business owners on Mayor Antonio Villaraigosa's Trade Mission to Mexico. I was especially proud to represent NAWBO-LA and the larger Los Angeles business community as a Latina woman who believes that the best way to promote entrepreneurship globally is to "build bridges" between and across borders and businesses. (www.nawbola.org)

## U.S. Patent and Trademark Office

Patents, trademarks, and copyrights are three types of intellectual property protection. They are different and serve different purposes. Patents protect inventions, and improvements to existing inventions.

Trademarks include any word, name, symbol, or device, or any combination, used, or intended to be used in commerce to identify and distinguish the goods of one manufacturer or seller from goods manufactured or sold by others, and to indicate the source of the goods. Service marks include any word, name, symbol, device, or any combination, used, or intended to be used in commerce to identify and distinguish the services of one provider from services provided by others, and to indicate the source of the services. Copyrights protect literary, artistic, and musical works. For general information, publications and other copyright-related topics, you may visit their Web site at http://www.copyright.gov.

## Educational Help

There's no question that that there are many available educational programs that are designed to help entrepreneurs grow. For example, Babson College in Maryland has some of the highest-rated programs. There is also Walton, at the University of Pensylvania; Kellogg at Northwestern; Darden at the University of Virginia; and California State University in Fullerton. Other examples of community colleges include Rancho Santiago Community College in Orange County, California; Santa Monica College in Santa Monica, California, and so on.

There are programs available at universities where they provide company reviews for established businesses. Once you have been in business for some years, you can contact your local university, specifically their small-business institute. In 1997, Cal State Fullerton (www.fullerton.edu) contacted me and offered me a complete review of the company made by five MBA candidates. The review took about three months. At the end, they provided us with a full report and recommendations for the company. Ten years later, Cal State Fullerton did another Consulting Report for Lulu's Dessert covering the areas of marketing, financial review, human resources, accounting review, operations review, and summary of recommendations.

The difference between such a review and a professional consulting firm is great. This is a win-win situation for the students and the university and Lulu's Dessert. I highly recommend that you contact your local university and find a similar program. For further information, you can contact Michael D. Ames, Ph.D., at Cal State Fullerton.

There are many other resources available for entrepreneurs. This chapter was a sampling of what I have found useful. Take advantage of all the great resources that are out there. Some were not available when I first started my businesses, but they would have been extremely helpful. Now that you know about them, use them as tools that will aid you in reaching the success for which you strive.

# Chapter 14:
# Conclusion

We hope that these stories have not only inspired you, but have taught you about thriving Latina entrepreneurs and their persistence in the face of great adversity and challenges. Their drive, their ambition, and their desire to fight is an inspiration to all of us.

In this book we have tried to translate the stories into actionable lessons that you can immediately put to work in your business and personal life.

Each of these women created her business from a desire and a dream, finding a niche with the capital and resources she had and thus made her dream a reality. They shared how they integrated their business into their lives while balancing family, education, relationships, health issues, and personal growth.

The eight stories profiled in this book should enable you to recognize and contemplate some of the options you have.

Think about all the most common themes that enabled each one of the entrepreneurs to succeed, for example:

All of them demonstrated ethical behavior, honesty dealing with customers, brokers, banks, partners, employees, and suppliers. Some found working with men very difficult at the beginning, but they eventually found a way to gain their respect. They learned how to negotiate insurmountable challenges, went through entreprene-urial abuse, and many of them broke down and cried many times. There was also the divorce factor combined with the hardest part of being a mother and fighting for child custody. There were language barriers and finally, a brain aneurism that made one look at life from a different prospective. But all had to become stronger in spirit and strive for power. All of them used the challenges as part of making their business grow and learned more about themselves in order to reinvent their lives and companies.

They have demonstrated that mentoring is a great way to find support; you don't have to do it by yourself, build a team around you and use resources starting with your own family.

I have always said that there is tremendous talent in our Latino community; there is something special in our culture that makes us natural risk takers and contributors to our communities-*determinación*. Let's all make a difference in whatever position we have by supporting each other. Have the courage to take risks, and be prepared to live with the consequences. Not every entre-preneur will be successful; many run out of time, money or can't find enough customers. Not everything is within our control, we all depend on what competitors do, change of markets, high cost of operations, new regulations, the weather, and the world economy. We all do the best we can with our resources.

Now it is your turn to start taking action. It is your time to develop a market and an innovative product or service to make a difference in people's lives and our economy. It is your time to create something from nothing that is built to last, just like we did. The Hispanic/Latino market has very promising opportunities and is expanding itself constantly. It is your money, time, and effort you are investing. You need to protect your investment and be smart about the decisions you make. You have the tools, start working now!

# Appendix

Here are some more valuable sources you will find helpful:

## Magazines

Entrepreneur Magazine
www.entrepreneur.com

Fortune Magazine
www.fortune.com

Hispanic Business Magazine
www.hispanicbusiness.com

Inc. Magazine
www.inc.com

Latin Business Magazine
www.latinbusinessmag.com

Latina Style Magazine
www.latinastyle.com

Latin Trade Magazine
www.latintrade.com

Tu Dinero Magazine
www.editorialtelevisa.us

## Networking/Counseling

California State University, Fullerton
www.fullerton.edu

Center for Women's Business Research
www.nfwbo.org

Counselors to America's Small Business
www.score.org

Enterprising Women Exhibit
www.radcliffe.edu/schles/exhibits/enterprisingwomen

Forum for Women Entrepreneurs & Executives
www.fwe.org

Hispanic Business Consultants- Eduardo Figueroa
www.eduardofigueroa.com

Institute for Women Entrepreneurs, Orange County
www.ociwe.com

Latina Style
www.latinastyle.com

Latina Style Business Series
http://bs.latinastyle.com/

MANA- A National Latina Organization
www.hermana.org

National Business Women Association
www.nlbwa.com

NAWBO- National Association of Women Business Owners
www.nawbo.org

NAWBO-LA- National Association of Women Business Owners, Los Angeles Chapter
www.nawbola.org

NBIA: National Business Incubation Association
www.nbia.org

NHBWA: National Hispanic Business Women Association
www.nationalhbwa.org

Online Women's Business Center
www.onlinewbc.org

Score- Counselors to America's Small Business of Orange County
www.score114.org

Small Business Administration
www.sba.gov

WBENC: The Women's Business Enterprise National Council
www.wbenc.org

Women Business Owners
www.wbo.ca

Women Business Owners
www.womenbizowners.org

Women Business Owners
www.womenbusinessowners.org

Women's Business Grants
www.usagovernmentgrants.org

Women Entrepreneurs
www.women-business-owners.org

Women's Leadership Exchange
www.womensleadershipexchange.com

## Certifications

National Women Business Owners Corporation Certification
www.nwboc.org

Small Business and DVBE Certification
www.pd.dgs.ca.gov/smbus

## Funding Sources

Active Capital
www.activecapital.org

Angel Capital Association
www.angelcapitalassociation.com

Investors' Circle
www.investorscircle.net

Microlending organizations
www.microenterpriseworks.org

Nacional Financiera
www.nafin.com

National Association of Seed and Venture Funds
www.nasvf.org

National Association of Small Business Investment Companies
www.nasbic.org

National Venture Capital Association
www.nvca.org

Quicken Small Business
www.quicken.com/small_business

Small Business Administration
www.sba.gov/financing/basics

Venture Capitalists
www.startupnation.com

Western Association of Venture Capitalists
www.wavc.net

## Entrepreneurs' Sources

American National Standards Institute
www.ansi.org

American Society of Association Executives (list of associations)
www.asaenet.org

Association of Small Business Development centers
www.asbdc-us.org

Better Business Bureaus
www.bbb.org
www.bbbonline.org

Bulletin Board: iVillage
www.ivillage.com

The Digital Media Center
www.dmc-works.com

Entrepreneurial Edge
www.edwardlowe.org

Entreworld
www.entreworld.org

FWE: Forum for Women Entrepreneurs
www.fwe.org

Hoovers
www.hoovers.com

International Customs Brokerage Firm
www.ibius.com

Microsoft Small Business Center
www.microsoft.com/smallbusiness

NASE: National Association for the Self-Employed
www.nase.org

Small Business Administration District Office
www.sba.gov/localresources/index.html

The United Inventors Association
www.uiausa.org

United States Chamber of Commerce
www.uschamber.com

United States Small Business Administration
www.sba.gov

## Government Sources

Bureau of Labor Statistics
www.bls.gov

Federal Trade Commission
www.ftc.gov

Information on copyrights
www.copyright.gov

Small Business Tax ID Number
www.irs.gov/pub/irs-pdf/fss4.pdf

Tax Information for Starting a Business
www.irs.gov/businesses/index.html

United States Census Data
www.census.gov

United States Consumer Product Safety Commission
www.cpsc.gov

United States Customs and Border Protection
www.customs.gov

United States International Trade Commission
www.usitc.gov

United States Patent and Trademark Office
www.uspto.gov

United States Securities and Exchange Commission
www.sec.gov

## Useful Books

*The E-Myth Revisited: Why Most Small Businesses Don't Work and What to Do About It,* Michael E. Gerber

*Guerilla Marketing,* Jay Conrad Levinson

*The Mom Inventors Handbook,* Tamara Monosoff

*One Page Business Plan,* Jim Horan

*Profiting from Intellectual Capital: Extracting Value from Innovation,* Patrick H. Sullivan

# Index

# WIN WEALTH WORTH WITH WBUSINESS BOOKS

## Sales

First 100 Days of Selling: A Practical
Day-by-Day Guide to Excel in the
Sales Profession
ISBN 13: 978-0-8329-5004-9

By Jim Ryerson

Price: $22.95 USD

Great Salespeople Aren't Born,
They're Hired: The Secrets to Hiring
Top Sales Professionals
ISBN 13: 978-0-8329-5000-1

By Joe Miller

Price: $19.95 USD

Hire, Fire, & the Walking Dead:
A Leaders Guide to Recruiting the Best
ISBN 13: 978-0-8329-5001-8

By Greg Moran with
Patrick Longo
Price: $19.95 USD

Soar Despite Your Dodo Sales Manager
ISBN 13: 978-0-8329-5009-4

By Lee B. Salz
Price: $19.95 USD

## Marketing

What's Your BQ? Learn How 35 Companies
Add Customers, Subtract Competitors, and
Multiply Profits with Brand Quotient
ISBN 13: 978-0-8329-5002-5

By Sandra Sellani

Price: $24.95 USD

Reality Sells: How to Bring Customers
Back Again and Again by Marketing
Your Genuine Story
ISBN 13: 978-0-8329-5008-7

By Bill Guertin and
Andrew Corbus

Price: $19.95 USD

## Entrepreneurship

The N Factor: How Efficient Networking
Can Change the Dynamics of Your Business
ISBN 13: 978-0-8329-5006-3

By Adrie Reinders and
Marion Freijsen
Price: $19.95 USD

Millionaire by 28
ISBN 13: 978-0-8329-5010-0

By Todd Babbitt
Price: $19.95 USD

Check out these books at your local bookstore or at
www.Wbusinessbooks.com

# THIS BOOK DOESN'T END AT THE LAST PAGE!

## We Want to hear from you!

Log on to **www.WBusinessBooks.com** and join the WBusiness community.

Share your thoughts, talk to the author, and learn from other community members in the forums. **www.WBusinessBooks.com** is a place you can sharpen your skills, learn the new trends and network with other sales professionals.